TWENTIETH CENTURY INTERPRETATIONS
OF

OEDIPUS REX

(Sophocles, 497/496 B.C. - 406/405)

A Collection of Critical Essays

Edited by

Michael J. O'Brien

Prentice-Hall, Inc. *Englewood Cliffs, N. J.*

A SPECTRUM BOOK

To M.E.O'B. and M.J.O'B.

Current printing (last number):

10 9 8 7 6 5

Prentice-Hall International, Inc. (*London*)

Contents

TWENTIETH CENTURY INTERPRETATIONS

OF

OEDIPUS REX

Introduction

by Michael J. O'Brien

About the life of Sophocles there exists a modest amount of information almost none of which is of any help in the interpretation of his plays. He was born in 497/496 B.C. and died in 406/405. Living as he did through most of the fifth century, he saw in succession the Persian invasions of Greece and their defeat, the growth of Athens as an imperial power and center of culture under the regime of Pericles, and the long, cruel, ruinous war with Sparta and her allies which began in 431 and was drawing to a close when he died. He was a native of Colonus, on the outskirts of Athens, where a local cult honored the hero Oedipus, said to have been buried there. Apart from that fact there are almost no grounds for a literary biography that would connect the events of Sophocles' own life with the inspiration of his tragedies or the growth of his art. Rich, successful, sociable, witty, and long-lived, he gives even less comfort than does Shakespeare to the biographical and psychological schools of literary criticism. We know of no personal sorrow that sparked the composition of the play we call *Oedipus Rex* or *Oedipus Tyrannus*, and attempts to link it with public disasters like the plague of Athens are not entirely convincing. His art in some ways, however, clearly shows the influence of fifth-century thought; the portrayal of Oedipus in particular reflects an awareness of the language and attitudes of the fifth-century Enlightenment.[1] He was a prolific writer and one highly acclaimed during his own lifetime. At his first appearance in dramatic competition, in 468, he won the victory, and he went on to win a disproportionately large number of victories after that. To our surprise, one of his occasional defeats is said to have occurred the year he presented the *Oedipus Rex*. Several technical innovations in theatrical art are attributed to him, including the introduction of scene painting and the use of scenes involving three speaking parts; and he is said to have written a treatise on his art. He found time as well to hold several high public offices and to serve as a priest of a minor healing-god. He was honored by those who knew him for his charm and his good temper.

[1] See Bernard M. W. Knox, *Oedipus at Thebes* (New Haven and London, 1957), pp. 107-58.

1

Of the more than one hundred twenty plays of Sophocles known to antiquity only seven tragedies have survived intact into modern times. Not all of these can be dated with confidence. An ancient anecdote would date the *Antigone* to about 442, and the *Ajax* is generally placed somewhat earlier, for reasons of style. The *Philoctetes* is known to have been produced in 409 and the *Oedipus at Colonus* in 401, the latter posthumously. The dates of the *Women of Trachis,* the *Electra,* and the *Oedipus Rex* are uncertain, but there are some grounds for dating the last-named play to the years immediately following 430. Three of his extant plays deal with the legend of the Theban royal house, the two *Oedipus* plays and the *Antigone.* The main outlines of this legend he inherited. The *Iliad* and the *Odyssey* both allude briefly to Oedipus, and two lost epics, the *Oedipodeia* and the *Thebaid,* were more directly concerned with his story. In the fifth century both Aeschylus and Euripides wrote Oedipus plays, neither of which survives. In later ages the theme has attracted numerous playwrights, Seneca, Corneille, Voltaire, Cocteau, and Gide among them, and even, it appears, the occasional amateur like Julius Caesar. But in most minds the names of Oedipus and Sophocles are inseparably linked.

To call the *Oedipus Rex* a play of inexhaustible interest is not to lapse into the customary hyperboles of authors of introductions. Literary critics and students of Greek religion continue in our century to turn to it, not to mention the anthropologists and psychologists, who find it useful as a reflection of primeval myth and man's unconscious mind. The present volume is a small testimony to the advances in our understanding of it made in the last six or seven decades alone. It remains a subject of intense discussion. Some things about it are clearer than others and are relatively safe ground for the scholar. These have to do with the way it works as a piece of stagecraft and with the methods used to engage the interest and excite the emotions of the audience. On the other hand, the question of the play's meaning is embroiled in seemingly hopeless controversy.

Most of the essays in this volume confine themselves mainly to one or the other of these two large topics: Sophocles' dramatic craftsmanship and Sophoclean thought. The clearest example of an essay of the first type is Owen's (*see* p. 30), since it is in fact based on the theory that the essence of drama-making is to be sought in the way the poet works on his audience. For different reasons, Lattimore's analysis of the story pattern (p. 41) and Kirkwood's discussion of character portrayal (p. 67) might also fall into this general category. Most of the essays, however, and almost all the short selections gathered in View Points are devoted to the play's meaning. The nine essays were chosen with an eye to quality and variety, and as a group they embody some serious differences of interpretation. The reader will find that a single point of view has not been imposed on him and that some things have been left to his judgment. Immense differences of interpretation can be found in the section called View Points. The purpose of this part of the book is to show in how many different places Sophoclean meaning has been found to lie: not only in religious ritual and in the intellectual life of the fifth century B.C., but in the moral law, in the unconscious, and in the dialectic of history. Not many men have dismissed this play as inconsequential or inferior, like Voltaire and Paul Shorey. Fewer still have contented themselves, like Longinus, with a simple expression of the highest praise. Most have found profound meaning in the play, and they have given us a diversity of interpretation that ranges from the engaging didacticism of Plutarch to the more somber and complex explanations of the twentieth century: Freudian, post-Freudian, Marxist, existentialist, and McLuhanist. View Points does not attempt to do justice to all of these, since limitations of space have often prevented the inclusion of supporting argument. But the interested reader who has the use of a library can always look further into those interpretations that recommend themselves to him.

The two questions to be asked about the *Oedipus Rex,* then, are, "How does it work as a play?" and "What does it all mean?" In this introduction I shall have more to say about the second than about the first. It is not obvious that the two can in fact be separated in practice, but many critics ask only one or the other rather than both, and the distinction is useful as a starting point for discussion. To refuse to go beyond the first question would be to take the position of those who say that Sophocles was "simply a dramatist" or "above all a dramatist." When phrases of this type are used in polemic they have an Occamist flavor: they suggest that the speaker is rejecting unsubstantial and unverifiable hypotheses about higher meanings and sticking to the known fact that Sophocles was writing to please an audience. The implication is that the events and the characters in his plays are irreducibly particular, that the former are not meant to be typical of human life or the latter of human nature. The audience watching the *Oedipus Rex*—if we follow this view—is meant to be absorbed by the rich detail of incident and characterization, music and poetic imagery, all cunningly arranged by a master playwright. The critic who sees the *Oedipus Rex* in this light will confine his discussion of it to plot construction, character portrayal, poetic imagery, and the like. All of these he will regard as safe and proper subjects, since they concern the play's relation to itself. But caution and diffidence will seize him when he is asked what relation the play or its parts bear to the world outside the play, what Sophocles is trying to say about fifth-century Athens or about human life. That way, he will answer, lies the ultimate reduction of a work of art to allegory and sermonizing. "The idea of the

drama is the play itself, not something that can be extracted from it,"
as E. T. Owen puts it near the beginning of his essay. A. J. A. Waldock announces a similar view with a more uncompromising turn of
phrase: "There is no meaning in the *Oedipus Tyrannus*." [2]

But the Occamists do not hold the field. Far from it. Most critics
who discuss this play assume that Sophocles put his whole soul and his
deepest convictions into it, that he was trying to "say something" and
not merely trying to enthrall the audience. Far from being identical
with "the play itself" as opposed to "something that can be extracted
from it," what he has said, they believe, lies waiting to be extracted. At
this point we are no longer in the theater with Owen and Waldock,
engrossed in a drama which is its own meaning, but in the library with
Bowra, who says of Sophocles, "It is . . . legitimate to ask what is the
real meaning of his plays, what general truths are embodied in his
particular presentations, and what, if any, was his own opinion about
them." [3] Bowra would see the primary meaning of the *Oedipus Rex*
and of Sophocles' other plays in certain lessons they teach about morally desirable attitudes and behavior, but of course this is not the only
kind of statement that a play can make about the outside world. It is
a priori quite possible—always assuming such an outside reference—
that the *Oedipus Rex* is about Athens of the 420's B.C. but not about
human life in general. It is possible too that its portrait of fifth-century Athens or of human life is disinterested and descriptive and implies no social or moral precepts. The choice of any of these possibilities would be an assertion that the play "says something"—and not
only something about Oedipus and legendary Thebes.

The most readily understandable form of this theory is that the
Oedipus Rex is a lesson and Sophocles is a teacher. The main evidence
for this is not so much the play itself, which unfortunately delivers
quite opposite lessons to different readers, but rather the general demands which Greek culture is alleged to have laid on its playwrights
and other poets. "In the fifth century," says T. B. L. Webster roundly,
"the poet was regarded as a teacher"; and Werner Jaeger has told us
that "The Greeks always felt that a poet was in the broadest and deepest sense the educator of his people." [4] There is, admittedly, a good
deal of ancient evidence to support this view, both in what poets say
themselves and in what others say about them. The sophist Protagoras
(if we can believe Plato's report at 316d of the dialogue named after
him) counted Homer, Hesiod, Simonides, Orpheus, and Musaeus

---

[2] A. J. A. Waldock, *Sophocles the Dramatist* (Cambridge, 1966), p. 168.
[3] C. M. Bowra, *Sophoclean Tragedy* (Oxford, 1944), p. 6.
[4] T. B. L. Webster, *An Introduction to Sophocles* (Oxford, 1936), p. 18; Werner
Jaeger, *Paideia: The Ideals of Greek Culture*, trans. Gilbert Highet, 3rd English ed.
(Oxford, 1946), I, 35.

among the professional educators. As he put it, they were all really sophists like himself but, fearing opprobrium, called themselves poets or prophets. Among authors of tragedies, Euripides was accused by his detractors of teaching atheism. The dealer in religious articles in Aristophanes' comedy *Thesmophoriazusae* (443 ff.) who attacks Euripides for having ruined her business has no doubt that he is a teacher and a bad one. In another of his comedies, the *Frogs,* Aristophanes stages a contest in Hades between the two dead tragic poets Aeschylus and Euripides, and one of the rules they agree on is that a poet should make his fellow citizens better men (1009–10). In the next century, as readers of the *Republic* know, Plato paid oblique tribute to the influence of the poet-teacher by proposing that in the ideal state he be brought under rigid political control.

The actual practice of Greek poets supports to some extent what others say about their teaching intent. Hesiod and Pindar do not shrink from pointing morals. Aeschylus' tragedy *The Eumenides* is heavy with commentary on the advantages of law and good political order. Indeed the use of an exemplary story to persuade the listener is a practice as old as Homer. The precedent for it is set by Phoenix in the ninth book of the *Iliad* when he tells the story of Meleager in order to teach Achilles the wisdom of accepting Agamemnon's offer of reconciliation. No one could fairly maintain that didacticism was absent from Greek literature. But that is not yet proof that the *Oedipus Rex* must be read—or even can be read—as a lesson. It is worth noting that, aside from some clearly didactic passages in contemporary poetry, the main evidence that Greeks of the fifth and early fourth centuries regarded the poet primarily as a teacher comes either from men whose own lives centered around education (like Plato and Protagoras) or from the comic author Aristophanes. But old comedy, of all forms of Greek poetry, is the one most deeply immersed in contemporary life and issues. The comic poet is no better qualified than the philosopher to interpret the tragic poet's intentions for us. We should like to have some evidence as to how Sophocles himself conceived of his purpose, but unfortunately we have nothing very informative.[5]

We are thrown back, therefore, on the play itself. One group of critics would have us search it for evidence of Sophocles' reaction to contemporary events and public personages and policies. It appears from the way this is sometimes practiced that one need not always keep the play as a whole in sharp focus. The isolated chorus and the single line often yield treasures of meaning to those who have an eye

---

[5] Sophocles' reported remark that he drew "men as they ought to be" need not imply didactic purpose. See C. M. Bowra, *Problems of Greek Poetry* (Oxford, 1953), pp. 122–24.

for covert allusion and a tolerant sense of what constitutes proof. But such criticism at its higher levels can be interesting and far-reaching. Victor Ehrenberg, in his book *Sophocles and Pericles,* has defended (with cautions and reservations) the theory that the personality of Oedipus reflects that of the Athenian leader Pericles, a man with whom Sophocles allegedly disagreed but whom he also admired. Ehrenberg, however, is aware of the difficulty of supposing that characters in a tragedy can conform to the internal order of the play and at the same time imitate real people; and his problems are compounded by his desire to see Pericles reflected as well in an earlier Sophoclean character who stands on a measurably lower moral plane, Creon of the *Antigone.* Moreover, Bernard Knox has gathered in much of the evidence used to identify Oedipus with Pericles and used it to defend the theory that Oedipus symbolizes (among other things) Athens itself.[6] I do not propose to go into this large and interesting question of what Sophocles thought of his contemporaries and their policies. One thing does seem clear, however. Ehrenberg has urged us not to be intimidated by "that towering bastion from which the literary critics dominate the intellectual and artistic countryside" and to try to see the poet as "a man speaking to his own people." [7] But few classicists are really intimidated by the ideal of pure literary criticism. On the contrary, the practice of relating Sophocles to his own world has continued undeterred in countless *obiter dicta* and in more substantial form by such recent authors as Whitman, Knox, and Ehrenberg himself.

The preferred ground, however, on which critics hunt for significance in the *Oedipus Rex* is the philosophical. If there is such a thing as "Sophoclean thought," then a more suitable subject than the ephemeral world of war and politics might seem to be the great problems of man's relationship to the gods and to fate. Plutarch tells us that good poetry is a preparation for philosophy, that it is in fact philosophy softened and mellowed for the benefit of those who cannot yet gaze with unshielded eyes upon the full blaze of truth.[8] His view still wins some measure of approval. H. D. F. Kitto has given us a book entitled *Sophocles, Dramatist and Philosopher.* Sir John Sheppard had earlier written *The Wisdom of Sophocles.* Sir Maurice Bowra has explained in the first chapter of his book *Sophoclean Tragedy* that the plays embody general truths which it is the business of the critic to discover and put into formulas. Sheppard, in his edition of the *Oedipus Rex,* has interpreted that play as illustrating the value of the vir-

[6] Victor Ehrenberg, *Sophocles and Pericles* (Oxford, 1954), pp. 148–49; Knox, *Oedipus at Thebes,* pp. 63–64.

[7] Ehrenberg, pp. 2, 7.

[8] Plutarch, *How the Young Man Should Study Poetry,* 35f–37b.

tue which the Greeks called *sophrosyne* and which we translate vari-
ously as modesty, temperance, or awareness of one's limitations. There
has been an inevitable revolt against the bland and pious figure that
has emerged from some of these interpretations bearing the title Sophocles the Thinker. "An enlightened bishop," said Cedric Whitman,
borrowing a tart phrase from E. M. Forster. But Whitman's iconoclasm
did not go so far as to reject the notion that Sophocles was a philosopher as well as a poet. He was simply to be a different kind of philosopher, one whose "metaphysic" reflected no conventional religiosity
but instead the dictum of Protagoras, his contemporary, that man is
the measure of all things. Hence the title of Whitman's book, *Sophocles, A Study of Heroic Humanism.*[9]

Enlightened bishop or heroic humanist: the author of the *Oedipus
Rex* can hardly be both; one begins to wonder whether he is either
one. The problem has two stages, which are not always clearly distinguished. First, is there a sense in which Oedipus represents man and
the events of the play represent human life? Second, if the play does
embody such a universal meaning, is the latter reducible to a set of
ethical precepts or even to a coherent system of moral values? The
answers I am inclined to give are Yes to the first and No to the second.
If they can be defended they will help explain the presence in critical
literature of diametrically opposed theories of the play's meaning, and
perhaps explain as well the insistence of a few critics that it has no
meaning at all.

The *Oedipus Rex,* in barest outline, is the story of a man's discovery, through persistent inquiry, that he is guilty of unwitting parricide
and incest, and his horrified reaction to that discovery. That Oedipus,
king of Thebes, had unknowingly killed his father and married his
mother was an ancient legend. But upon that rudimentary story Sophocles had the choice of imposing any pattern that he wished. The relationship of these two elements in the play, one traditional and the
other Sophoclean, is, roughly speaking, that between matter and form.
The legend, being partially preformed, may have meanings of its own
which it brings into the play. But any interpretation of the play, as
opposed to the legend, will be concerned mainly with what the play
makes important, not with what is merely implicit in the legend. What
is it, then, that distinguishes Sophocles' story from the many other
stories potentially present in the legendary material? There is the fact,
to begin with, that he has made his play an elaborate and sustained
exercise of intellect, an inquiry begun to solve one problem (Who
killed Laius?) which is then diverted to another problem (Who is
Oedipus?). Inquiry and discovery, to be sure, form a regular feature

---

[9] Published at Cambridge, Mass., 1951. See epigraph to Part One (p. 1), pp. 20,
228–29, and the title of Chapter XII, "The Metaphysic of Humanism."

of Greek tragedy, but nowhere else do they constitute virtually the entire play. Moreover, recognition is not normally the result of the efforts of a single character; instead, he can expect a certain amount of effective cooperation. The results in other plays are consequently not so striking as displays of intelligence or of energy. In this play the subordinate characters may supply information from time to time, but none cooperates effectively in evaluating it, and some of them, like Teiresias, Jocasta, and the Theban shepherd, actually resist. The plot, then, is not only a sustained act of intellect, but the act of one man's intellect.

What is true of the plot is also true of the way Oedipus himself is conceived. Though he is by no means a one-dimensional character, his various qualities are not of equal importance, nor do they have an equal place in his own conception of himself. His kingly benevolence, irascibility, and vigor are all on display, and each contributes to the development of the action, yet the only quality that becomes a major issue is his intelligence. A good illustration of how well plot, character, and thought are adapted to one another is given by the way in which the intelligence of Oedipus becomes a focus of discussion to a degree that his hot temper, for example, does not, in spite of several allusions to it. One can see this to best advantage in the Teiresias scene. In its broad outlines this scene is similar to many others in which wise counsellors confront impetuous kings, but in this play it has taken on a highly individual and appropriate form. As soon as the argument gets under way and the king begins his tirade against this prophet who will not help his city (380 ff.), it becomes clear that Sophocles has rejected as inappropriate several possible lines of development. That proud and angry speech, in which Oedipus attacks Teiresias and praises himself, might easily have turned on a contrast between selfishness and patriotism, or venality and incorruptibility, or feebleness and youthful vigor. Each of these themes is alluded to, but all are subordinated to the emphatic, repeated claim: You are inept and I am clever. (This will even recur as a minor theme in the Creon scene, at lines 536–42.) Nor would so much have been made of Teiresias' blindness had it not been for its promise of appropriate symbolism. His blindness is of no importance, and is hardly mentioned, in other plays in which he appears. Yet here Oedipus taunts him cruelly on account of it and adds that he is blind in his art as well (371, 374, 389). The ground is thus prepared for Teiresias' reply, that Oedipus is figuratively blind already and will one day be literally blind (372–73, 412–19). By the time Teiresias has pronounced his final oracle and has left the uncomprehending king trying to fathom its meaning, Oedipus' proud claim to have outwitted the Sphinx and his scorn for Teiresias' blindness have been rebuked in a doubly unexpected way. The prophet has used his blindness as the launching-point of his rebuttal, and he has baffled the quick-witted king with his oracles. Appropriately, his parting shot is a challenge to Oedipus' intelligence: "Go in and think that out!"

The question which the Teiresias scene thrusts to the foreground is not so much the hero's guilt or innocence as it is his power of understanding. It is this power, not his clear conscience, which seems the ground of Oedipus' self-esteem (as shown at line 441), and which nevertheless bears the main brunt of Teiresias' scorn. It is in the reproaches of Teiresias that the issue of what the king does and does not understand is first made explicit, but even before this scene it had been implied by ironic statement. That this play is full of remarks that mean one thing to the speaker but something else to the audience hardly needs proof or illustration. Irony of this kind, wherever it occurs in literature, will always imply that the speaker is unaware of something, but this implication need not be its main purpose. If an ironic remark simply foreshadows a disaster to come, then the ignorance of the speaker, indeed whether it is one speaker or another, need not count for anything. Such would be the effect, for example, if the messenger, not Oedipus, had ventured the remark at line 999. Even when irony serves as commentary on the speaker's character, it may direct our attention to his treachery, cowardice, or other faults rather than to his ignorance.[10] But when Oedipus says, "You are all sick but, sick as you are, there is none so sick as I" (60–61), and "I will fight on his behalf as if for my own father" (264–65), the words can only be meant to emphasize his profound unawareness of the truth.

Irony of this type, which begins to appear early in the play, is only the first step in the formation of a complex theme. Two further steps are the king's expression of self-confident wisdom and the gods' own claim to knowledge. Until the Teiresias scene Oedipus seems merely deluded; he is not yet a man who prides himself on his clear-sightedness. Moreover, until that scene there is nothing against which to measure his delusion, except, of course, that minimum prerequisite for the existence of irony, the knowing poet and his knowing audience. In the argument with Teiresias, however, the king himself provides us with another standard of comparison, the prophet's art. It is at first only Teiresias whose knowledge Oedipus claims he has surpassed, and his attitude might easily be confused with the common theme of indignation at individual venal and untrustworthy prophets. But later incidents keep the theme alive and gradually reveal that it involves a more fundamental challenge. Jocasta, to begin with, recalls an oracle about her child which did not come true and whose failure persuaded her that "nothing mortal has a share in the pro-

---

[10] This is a typically Euripidean effect. See *Medea* 489 and *Electra* 369–70.

phetic art" (709). She repeats her judgment against prophecy later
(857–58) as the one ray of light remaining at the end of an otherwise
harrowing conversation, during which Oedipus has realized that he
may have been the killer of Laius. The chorus, which had been only
moderately disturbed by the challenge to Teiresias, is profoundly
shocked by Jocasta's statements. It appears to them that if the old
oracles of Laius are discredited then Apollo's own claims and religion
itself are in question (906–910). The confrontation has become more
clearly one between Oedipus the "know-nothing" (to use his own
scornful, double-edged phrase of line 397) and Apollo. It is all very
well to say that Apollo is never directly challenged, that Jocasta continues to worship him, and that careful distinctions are maintained
between gods and their human representatives. The fact is that these
qualifications lose force and in the heat of argument come to be forgotten. Jocasta's choice of words at 853 ff. implies that she has refuted
Apollo himself. Later she cries "O oracles of the gods, where are you?"
when she is told that Polybus has died a natural death (946–47). "Listen and see what has become of the august oracles of the gods," she
adds a few lines later. Oedipus, catching her spirit, laughs at Delphi
and, as it appears, at prophecy in general (964–72); and when Jocasta
makes her famous speech on chance (977–83) the effect is to deny in
principle the power or willingness of the gods to predict man's future.
Therefore, she says, it is best to live at random. Oedipus, whose own
life has been spent in trying to evade an oracle, has begun to think—
and would be certain were it not for Merope's continued survival—
that he has won out. When the full truth comes out in the last episode
it appears that not only the knowing poet and his knowing audience
have relished the ironies of earlier scenes, but the gods have as well.

The plot of the *Oedipus Rex* is a search for knowledge, and its climax is a recognition of truth; the hero is a man whose self-esteem is
rooted in his pride of intellect; and the gods, those ever-present figures
in tragedy, rarely seen but always essential, manifest themselves here
not by thunderbolt or epiphany or sudden madness or miracle, but by
a prediction after long delay proved true. Various formulas have been
imposed on this play, according to the preferences of various critics.
Some of these, like "A wicked man is punished" or "An imprudent
man pays the price" have been based on a misreading of facts. Others,
like "A family curse returns" or "An innocent man is victimized by
fate" have involved a misjudgment of the play's central concern.[11] Better to call the play "A man matches wits with the gods." Formulas
should not be unduly honored, but this one, I think, has the advan-

[11] On these points I agree in the main with Dodds' essay and refer the reader to
it (*see* p. 17). See also the essays of Reinhardt (p. 49) and Winnington-Ingram
(p. 81).

tage of being suited to Sophocles' play. All of the others remain possible interpretations of the Oedipus legend and nothing more. That is, they sum up plays that might have been written by an author who used the principal facts of that legend as dramatic content.

"A man matches wits with the gods." We have to consider whether we can drop the indefinite article and raise the "m" in "man" to upper case. The main objections will come from those who stress the extraordinary particularity of what Oedipus does and suffers and suppose that this precludes any universal reference. One can begin to meet these objections by observing that the word "knowledge" is ambiguous as it applies to Oedipus. The knowledge he claims to have is the ability to solve riddles. Its connotations are mastery and power—the slain Sphinx, the throne of Thebes, and now perhaps the removal of the plague. On the other hand, the self-knowledge he achieves during the play has quite opposite implications. The ears of Athenians of the late fifth century would have been far better attuned than our own to this contrast. They were familiar with the controversial humanistic conception that man's knowledge, especially his technological and scientific knowledge, constituted his chief protection against disaster and his claim to greatness. That is a datum in the history of Greek language and culture.[12] Consequently, the posture Oedipus adopts before his fall, though it has been self-explanatory in all ages, belongs to a *type* of attitude especially familiar to them. On the other hand, his discovery of his own identity would also have had rather clearer associations in Sophocles' time than it does now. The play makes it evident that for Oedipus, if for no one else, self-knowledge is an appalling and a humbling experience. There is at first sight no universal meaning discernible here: Oedipus has had a singular past to learn about, and there will always be readers to say that this has nothing to do with them. But it would have reminded any Greek spectator of the maxim engraved at Delphi, which was attributed to more than one of the Seven Wise Men and had become a part of the popular wisdom: Know Thyself. There was, moreover, a commonly accepted way of understanding the phrase, viz. "Know your limitations, especially in relation to the gods, and stay within them." Self-knowledge is therefore understandably associated with the virtue of *sophrosyne,* a word usually best translated as modesty or self-restraint. The closer we look at the way Sophocles has organized his play, the less remote the story of Oedipus comes to seem from common Greek and common human concerns. As a man who in the flush of past achievement and present challenge seems to have cast off the burden of his human limitations and is then suddenly crushed under them, Oedipus is an example, however extreme, of what may happen to anyone. The chorus recognizes this im-

[12] See Knox, *Oedipus at Thebes,* pp. 107–10.

mediately: "Having your example (*paradeigma*), your fate, O wretched
Oedipus, I count nothing mortal blessed" (1193–96). In their eyes, at
this extraordinarily important moment in the play, Oedipus is not
primarily their king or their suffering friend (they will come to these
points later) but an example (*paradeigma*) of all mankind.

To call nothing mortal blessed comes very close to saying that no
man is a god, the gods being often called simply "the blessed ones."
We are reminded that in the second stasimon the chorus had drawn
the same contrast. The immediate occasion of their song had been
Jocasta's challenge to the truth of Apollo's oracle, which predicted
(falsely, she thought) that Laius would die at his son's hand. The
chorus had then placed her challenge, soon to be echoed by Oedipus,
against the background of the traditional measurement of man against
god. The gods and their laws are eternal and do not grow old. Man
is mortal; he grows old; and oblivion (*lethe*) in the long run will close
his eyes in sleep (863–72). Shakespeare thought of man as aging in
seven stages. The Greeks, in the riddle of the Sphinx, recognized three.
The Athenian of the fifth century knew the riddle well and could
have seen that both its content and its form had radically influenced
the shape of this play.[13] The riddle defines man as the one who
changes and grows old, a notion expressed in the imagery of the second stasimon, where it is a way of contrasting man and the eternal
gods; and it is cast in the form of an intellectual problem, and so is
the prototype of the more complex problem that confronts Oedipus
in the play. Once we realize this, it is not difficult to see reflections
of the riddle in the dramatic design. There are, one notices, occasional
reminders of the workings of time and of the passage from youth to
old age (e.g., at 17, 1082–83, 1112–13, 1145, 1213). All this, to be sure,
is conventional stuff: it is apt rather than striking. But there is one
person, Oedipus, the three stages of whose life are vividly presented to
us. The narrative of his adventures as a baby occupies the whole fourth
episode; we observe him ourselves at the height of his mature powers;
and through the medium of prophecy we glimpse his figure in old age,
three-footed, "pointing before him at the ground with his staff" (456).
The word the chorus uses to define the relation of Oedipus to mankind, *paradeigma*, seems appropriate as well to this changing visual
image. In his growth and decline, just as in his inability to outwit the
gods, he is not singular but typical of all men.

It is in the Teiresias scene that we can best see the influence of the
riddle as a poetic conception. It appears first in that scene as a mere
item of background information which, as it happens, serves Oedipus
well in his search for a line of argument. Where was Teiresias with

---

[13] *Ibid.*, p. 237, n. 31. See also Lattimore's essay.

his oracles when the Sphinx posed her riddle? "But *I* came and stopped her!" So far, it is merely a point scored against Teiresias and evidence for Oedipus' state of mind. But, like his other taunt, that Teiresias is blind, this one is soon turned back upon Oedipus with refined poetic justice. Teiresias, that is, begins to speak in riddles:

—This day shall see you born and shall destroy you.
—How everything you say is riddling and unclear beyond measure!
—Are you not the born expert at solving this sort of thing? (438–40)

The dart has been sunk, but Teiresias will not leave until he has justified fully the complaint of the king that he is being enigmatic. His last speech is cast in the form of a long riddle. The culprit is here in Thebes, an alien but a native; he will be blind, having had sight, and poor, having been rich; he will be brother and father to his own children, and son and husband to one woman; he will have sown with his father and killed him. This is the second riddle that Oedipus has been called upon to solve, and its effect is to define this whole play as the dramatization of a riddle and its solution. More complex than the old riddle, the new one nevertheless has a feature in common with it, that its subject ends his life three-footed (456). The most important link between them, however, is that when Oedipus discovers his own identity he learns about himself not only as an individual whose life story (as one author has put it) is a freak, an epigram in ill-luck; he also discovers what it is to be a man. That was also the lesson of the first riddle.

Now that the word "lesson" has reappeared, it must be faced squarely. The play appears to dramatize the conventional Greek wisdom that when ephemeral man vies with the deathless gods, the gods always win. The theme is as old as Homer, who tells the story of Lycurgus and Dionysus to illustrate it in the sixth book of the *Iliad*, 128 ff. In the *Oedipus Rex* the specific point of contention is knowledge. This is Sophocles' way of translating the old theme into a form suited to the age of the Enlightenment, and it creates a fine antithesis between knowledge as power and self-knowledge. In short, the awareness that man is less than the gods is undeniably an element in the play. Does that conventional wisdom, however, constitute the ultimate organizing principle of the play? Does the play mean "Know Thyself"? If we say it does, we shall find ourselves willy-nilly in the company of those who think that the play is a lesson and that Sophocles the poet is a teacher; for what the Delphic maxim just quoted amounts to is an admonition to cultivate *sophrosyne,* to be cautious, temperate, self-controlled, and always aware that man is shadow and vapor.

The most eloquent defender of the theory that the play teaches *sophrosyne,* Sheppard, has grasped the nettle firmly by declaring that

the touchstone by which Oedipus is to be judged is—Creon. Creon's
"pious moderation" and "modest loyalty" are the human ideals against
which the "arrogance" of Oedipus is measured and found wanting.[14]
Sheppard's critical instinct is perfectly sound in one respect. If the play
is designed to teach *sophrosyne,* then Creon's personality embodies the
values it recommends to us. Lest this fact should escape us, Creon
claims that virtue explicitly at line 589. He is at all times deferential,
cautious, and reverent. Even at the end, he insists that he will not ex-
pel Oedipus until he is absolutely sure that this is what the gods desire. It is he who points the obvious moral in the last scene, that now
perhaps Oedipus will put his faith in the gods. His last, minor dispute
with the king is over a question of *sophrosyne.* Oedipus wants to be
expelled immediately, but Creon will not promise it until the gods'
will is made quite clear. To make it plain that Creon is the antitype
of Oedipus in the latter's pride of knowledge, Sophocles makes him
utter twice a statement that we may take to be his motto: When I lack
knowledge I prefer to be silent (569, 1520). In one passage Creon elab-
orates his philosophy of life with larger strokes. What he reveals is a
desire to avoid the responsibilities of kingship because they are dangerous and painful, to be content instead with public approval and
honors that bring gain, and to be mindful of his subordinate place
(583–602). Creon is a just, even a kind, man. It is he who brings
the children on stage in the last scene, hoping to please Oedipus. He
is also an innocent man, unjustly accused, who reacts mildly and
seems not to bear a grudge at the end. But he is humdrum and poor-
spirited and self-satisfied. He is thoroughly decent in his way; but
Oedipus, with his boldness and intelligence and ease of command, is
splendid.

A similar contrast is evident between Oedipus and the other two
major characters who share scenes with him. Teiresias represents and
defends the wisdom of the gods in his opposition to human folly, but
as a person he does not measure up to the king. His first words in the
play show that he finds his knowledge unbearable, and he is quite prepared to turn about and go home until the king provokes him to anger.[15] Jocasta, on the other hand, for all her gentle and womanly virtues, has elevated irresponsibility to the status of a principle, and she
declares as much in her speech at lines 977–83. When she finally realizes the full truth, before Oedipus knows it, her nonchalance reappears, with terror behind it, in the bitterly twisted form of frantic

---

[14] J. T. Sheppard, ed., *The Oedipus Tyrannus of Sophocles* (Cambridge, 1920), pp.
lix–lxxix.
[15] There are good evaluations of Creon and Teiresias in J. C. Kamerbeek, ed.,
The Plays of Sophocles, Commentaries, Part IV: The Oedipus Tyrannus (Leiden,
1967), pp. 23, 106–7.

advice to pay no attention, to waste no more time in questions.[16] The reaction of the king at the moment of discovery will be quite different: "I am on the brink of hearing terrible things, but I must hear them." Neither Jocasta nor Teiresias is willing to face the truth, and Oedipus is. Neither Teiresias nor Creon wishes the responsibility that comes with power and office, and Oedipus does. Teiresias and Creon are both wiser men than he, and at the end of the play Creon is still giving him unheeded lessons in *sophrosyne*. But his brilliance and his courage make him a greater man than both of them.

There is no moral lesson here. It is not the way of a moralist to present human folly in such luminous colors while he paints wisdom and temperance in shades of gray. Nor does it save the argument to say that these are expedients of characterization meant to excite our sympathy for the hero, or to make his fall more impressive, or to avoid an artistic lapse into stereotypes of virtue and vice. That would only mean that to make a better play Sophocles had to make a worse lesson. But then the kind of play he was writing was intrinsically unsuited to be a lesson, and perhaps is not one at all. The play does not persuade us that Creon is a nobler man, only that he is a wiser man. It offers some comfort to the pious, but only a little, and it is designed to be a stumbling-block to philosophers like Plato, who believe in the unity of the virtues. On the other hand, so clear an illustration of a brilliant man's ignorance and vulnerability could not have much pleased the humanists of the fifth century, whose pride and faith in man's progress were based on their confidence in the power of his intellect. So long as we regard the play as a form of dramatized moral philosophy, we shall spend our energies trying to get beyond this dilemma. Our hope will be to determine once and for all whether Sophocles was at heart a religious conservative or a Protagorean humanist. It is a mistaken hope, for the play is not designed to give us an answer. Although it presents conflicting norms of value, it does not resolve their conflict in the sense of ranking them on a philosophic scale of better or worse. Instead it shows man at his noblest and greatest when he is most foolish, and in the very actions which exhibit his folly. We may accept that gratefully as a matchless artistic achievement, but we shall find in it no moral guidance.

A generation or so after the production of the *Oedipus Rex*, a drama was written on the subject of *sophrosyne* which is both philosophically coherent and didactically effective. This is Plato's *Charmides*, a prose dialogue in which the conflict is entirely verbal, but drama nonetheless. Its protagonist is Socrates, characterized as the man of self-knowledge and temperance. The work is so designed that we have no linger-

---

[16] There is even a verbal echo in line 1056 (*meden entrapes*) of line 724 (*entrepou su meden*).

ing admiration for Critias, his chief antagonist in argument and his antitype, a man both intemperate and unable to recognize the limits of his own knowledge. The *Charmides* is not so great a drama as the *Oedipus Rex,* but it is a better lesson. But then Plato was a philosopher rather than a poet. It is a distinction well worth keeping in mind.

PART ONE

Interpretations

On Misunderstanding the *Oedipus Rex*[1]

by E. R. Dodds

On the last occasion when I had the misfortune to examine in Honour Moderations at Oxford I set a question on the *Oedipus Rex,* which was among the books prescribed for general reading. My question was "In what sense, if in any, does the *Oedipus Rex* attempt to justify the ways of God to man?" It was an optional question; there were plenty of alternatives. But the candidates evidently considered it a gift: nearly all of them attempted it. When I came to sort out the answers I found that they fell into three groups.

The first and biggest group held that the play justifies the gods by showing—or, as many of them said, "proving"—that we get what we deserve. The arguments of this group turned upon the character of Oedipus. Some considered that Oedipus was a bad man: look how he treated Creon—naturally the gods punished him. Others said "No, not altogether bad, even in some ways rather noble; but he had one of those fatal ἁμαρτίαι that all tragic heroes have, as we know from Aristotle. And since he had a ἁμαρτία[2] he could of course expect no mercy: the gods had read the *Poetics*." Well over half the candidates held views of this general type.

A second substantial group held that the *Oedipus Rex* is "a tragedy of destiny." What the play "proves," they said, is that man has no free will but is a puppet in the hands of the gods who pull the strings that make him dance. Whether Sophocles thought the gods justified in treating their puppet as they did was not always clear from their answers. Most of those who took this view evidently disliked the play; some of them were honest enough to say so.

"*On Misunderstanding the* Oedipus Rex" *by E. R. Dodds. From* Greece and Rome, *XIII (1966), 37–49. Copyright © 1966 by the Clarendon Press, Oxford. Reprinted by permission of the publisher.*

[1] A paper read at a "refresher course" for teachers, London Institute of Education, 24 July 1964.

[2] Transliterated "hamartia." Dodds discusses its meaning below [*Editor's note*].

The third group was much smaller, but included some of the more thoughtful candidates. In their opinion Sophocles was "a pure artist" and was therefore not interested in justifying the gods. He took the story of Oedipus as he found it, and used it to make an exciting play. The gods are simply part of the machinery of the plot.

Ninety per cent of the answers fell into one or the other of these three groups. The remaining ten per cent had either failed to make up their minds or failed to express themselves intelligibly.

It was a shock to me to discover that all these young persons, supposedly trained in the study of classical literature, could read this great and moving play and so completely miss the point. For all the views I have just summarized are in fact demonstrably false (though some of them, and some ways of stating them, are more crudely and vulgarly false than others). It is true that each of them has been defended by some scholars in the past, but I had hoped that all of them were by now dead and buried. Wilamowitz thought he had killed the lot in an article published in *Hermes* (34 [1899], 55 ff.) more than half a century ago; and they have repeatedly been killed since. Yet their unquiet ghosts still haunt the examination-rooms of universities—and also, I would add, the pages of popular handbooks on the history of European drama. Surely that means that we have somehow failed in our duty as teachers?

It was this sense of failure which prompted me to attempt once more to clear up some of these ancient confusions. If the reader feels—as he very well may—that in this paper I am flogging a dead horse, I can only reply that on the evidence I have quoted the animal is unaccountably still alive.

I

I shall take Aristotle as my starting point, since he is claimed as the primary witness for the first of the views I have described. From the thirteenth chapter of the *Poetics* we learn that the best sort of tragic hero is a man highly esteemed and prosperous who falls into misfortune because of some serious (μεγάλη) ἁμαρτία: examples, Oedipus and Thyestes. In Aristotle's view, then, Oedipus' misfortune was directly occasioned by some serious ἁμαρτία; and since Aristotle was known to be infallible, Victorian critics proceeded at once to look for this ἁμαρτία. And so, it appears, do the majority of present-day undergraduates.

What do they find? It depends on what they expect to find. As we all know, the word ἁμαρτία is ambiguous: in ordinary usage it is some-

times applied to false moral judgements, sometimes to purely intellectual error—the average Greek did not make our sharp distinction between the two. Since *Poetics* 13 is in general concerned with the moral
character of the tragic hero, many scholars have thought in the past
(and many undergraduates still think) that the ἁμαρτία of Oedipus
must in Aristotle's view be a moral fault. They have accordingly gone
over the play with a microscope looking for moral faults in Oedipus,
and have duly found them—for neither here nor anywhere else did
Sophocles portray that insipid and unlikely character, the man of perfect virtue. Oedipus, they point out, is proud and over-confident; he
harbours unjustified suspicions against Teiresias and Creon; in one
place (lines 964 ff.) he goes so far as to express some uncertainty about
the truth of oracles. One may doubt whether this adds up to what
Aristotle would consider μεγάλη ἁμαρτία. But even if it did, it would
have no direct relevance to the question at issue. Years before the action of the play begins, Oedipus was already an incestuous parricide;
if that was a punishment for his unkind treatment of Creon, then the
punishment preceded the crime—which is surely an odd kind of justice.

"Ah," says the traditionalist critic, "but Oedipus' behaviour on the
stage reveals the man he always was: he was punished for his basically
unsound character." In that case, however, someone on the stage ought
to tell us so: Oedipus should repent, as Creon repents in the *Antigone*;
or else another speaker should draw the moral. To ask about a character in fiction "Was he a good man?" is to ask a strictly meaningless
question: since Oedipus never lived we can answer neither "Yes" nor
"No." The legitimate question is "Did Sophocles intend us to think of
Oedipus as a good man?" This *can* be answered—not by applying
some ethical yardstick of our own, but by looking at what the characters in the play say about him. And by that test the answer is "Yes."
In the eyes of the Priest in the opening scene he is the greatest and
noblest of men, the saviour of Thebes who with divine aid rescued the
city from the Sphinx. The Chorus has the same view of him: he has
proved his wisdom, he is the darling of the city, and never will they
believe ill of him (504 ff.). And when the catastrophe comes, no one
turns round and remarks "Well, but it was your own fault: it must
have been; Aristotle says so."

In my opinion, and in that of nearly all Aristotelian scholars since
Bywater, Aristotle does *not* say so; it is only the perversity of moralizing critics that has misrepresented him as saying so. It is almost certain
that Aristotle was using ἁμαρτία here as he uses ἁμάρτημα in the *Nico-
machean Ethics* (1135ᵇ12) and in the *Rhetoric* (1374ᵇ6), to mean an
offense committed in ignorance of some material fact and therefore

free from πονηρία [wickedness] or κακία. [vice].[3] These parallels seem decisive; and they are confirmed by Aristotle's second example—Thyestes, the man who ate the flesh of his own children in the belief that it was butcher's meat, and who subsequently begat a child on his own daughter, not knowing who she was. His story has clearly much in common with that of Oedipus, and Plato as well as Aristotle couples the two names as examples of the gravest ἁμαρτία (Laws 838c). Thyestes and Oedipus are both of them men who violated the most sacred of Nature's laws and thus incurred the most horrible of all pollutions; but they both did so without πονηρία, for they knew not what they did— in Aristotle's quasi-legal terminology, it was a ἁμάρτημα, not an ἀδίκημα [unjust act]. That is why they were in his view especially suitable subjects for tragedy. Had they acted knowingly, they would have been inhuman monsters, and we could not have felt for them that pity which tragedy ought to produce. As it is, we feel both pity, for the fragile estate of man, and terror, for a world whose laws we do not understand. The ἁμαρτία of Oedipus did not lie in losing his temper with Teiresias; it lay quite simply in parricide and incest—a μεγάλη ἁμαρτία indeed, the greatest a man can commit.

The theory that the tragic hero must have a grave moral flaw, and its mistaken ascription to Aristotle, has had a long and disastrous history. It was gratifying to Victorian critics, since it appeared to fit certain plays of Shakespeare. But it goes back much further, to the seventeenth-century French critic Dacier, who influenced the practice of the French classical dramatists, especially Corneille, and was himself influenced by the still older nonsense about "poetic justice"—the notion that the poet has a moral duty to represent the world as a place where the good are always rewarded and the bad are always punished. I need not say that this puerile idea is completely foreign to Aristotle and to the practice of the Greek dramatists; I only mention it because on the evidence of those Honour Mods. papers it would appear that it still lingers on in some youthful minds like a cobweb in an unswept room.

To return to the Oedipus Rex, the moralist has still one last card to play. Could not Oedipus, he asks, have escaped his doom if he had been more careful? Knowing that he was in danger of committing parricide and incest, would not a really prudent man have avoided quarreling, even in self-defence, with men older than himself, and also love-relations with women older than himself? Would he not, in Waldock's ironic phrase, have compiled a handlist of all the things he must not do? In real life I suppose he might. But we are not entitled to blame

---

[3] For the full evidence see O. Hey's exhaustive examination of the usage of these words, Philol. 83 (1927), 1–17; 137–63. Cf. also K. von Fritz, Antike und Moderne Tragödie (Berlin, 1962), 1 ff.

Oedipus either for carelessness in failing to compile a handlist or for lack of self-control in failing to obey its injunctions. For no such possibilities are mentioned in the play, or even hinted at; and it is an essential critical principle that *what is not mentioned in the play does not exist.* These considerations would be in place if we were examining the conduct of a real person. But we are not: we are examining the intentions of a dramatist, and we are not entitled to ask questions that the dramatist did not intend us to ask. There is only one branch of literature where we *are* entitled to ask such questions about τὰ ἐκτὸς τοῦ δράματος [what lies outside the action], namely the modern detective story. And despite certain similarities the *Oedipus Rex* is not a detective story but a dramatized folktale. If we insist on reading it as if it were a law report we must expect to miss the point.[4]

In any case, Sophocles has provided a conclusive answer to those who suggest that Oedipus could, and therefore should, have avoided his fate. The oracle was *unconditional* (line 790): it did not say "If you do so-and-so you will kill your father"; it simply said "You will kill your father, you will sleep with your mother." And what an oracle predicts is bound to happen. Oedipus does what he can to evade his destiny: he resolves never to see his supposed parents again. But it is quite certain from the first that his best efforts will be unavailing. Equally unconditional was the original oracle given to Laius (711 ff.): Apollo said that he *must* (χρῆναι) die at the hands of Jocasta's child; there is no saving clause. Here there is a significant difference between Sophocles and Aeschylus. Of Aeschylus' triology on the House of Laius only the last play, the *Septem,* survives. Little is known of the others, but we do know, from *Septem* 742 ff., that according to Aeschylus the oracle given to Laius *was* conditional: "Do not beget a child; for *if* you do, that child will kill you." In Aeschylus the disaster *could* have been avoided, but Laius sinfully disobeyed and his sin brought ruin to his descendants. In Aeschylus the story was, like the *Oresteia,* a tale of crime and punishment; but Sophocles chose otherwise—that is why he altered the form of the oracle. There is no suggestion in the *Oedi-*

---

[4] The danger is exemplified by Mr. P. H. Vellacott's article, "The Guilt of Oedipus," which appeared in this journal (vol. xi [1964], 137–48) shortly after my talk was delivered. By treating Oedipus as an historical personage and examining his career from the "common-sense" standpoint of a prosecuting counsel Mr. Vellacott has no difficulty in showing that Oedipus must have guessed the true story of his birth long before the point at which the play opens—and guiltily done nothing about it. Sophocles, according to Mr. Vellacott, realized this, but unfortunately could not present the situation in these terms because "such a conception was impossible to express in the conventional forms of tragedy"; so for most of the time he reluctantly fell back on "the popular concept of an innocent Oedipus lured by Fate into a disastrous trap." We are left to conclude either that the play is a botched compromise or else that the common sense of the law-courts is not after all the best yardstick by which to measure myth.

pus Rex that Laius sinned or that Oedipus was the victim of an hereditary curse, and the critic must not assume what the poet has abstained from suggesting. Nor should we leap to the conclusion that Sophocles left out the hereditary curse because he thought the doctrine immoral; apparently he did not think so, since he used it both in the *Antigone* (583 ff.) and in the *Oedipus at Colonus* (964 ff.). What his motive may have been for ignoring it in the *Oedipus Rex* we shall see in a moment.

I hope I have now disposed of the moralizing interpretation, which has been rightly abandoned by the great majority of contemporary scholars. To mention only recent works in English, the books of Whitman, Waldock, Letters, Ehrenberg, Knox, and Kirkwood, however much they differ on other points, all agree about the essential moral innocence of Oedipus.

II

But what is the alternative? If Oedipus is the innocent victim of a doom which he cannot avoid, does this not reduce him to a mere puppet? Is not the whole play a "tragedy of destiny" which denies human freedom? This is the second of the heresies which I set out to refute. Many readers have fallen into it, Sigmund Freud among them;[5] and you can find it confidently asserted in various popular handbooks, some of which even extend the assertion to Greek tragedy in general —thus providing themselves with a convenient label for distinguishing Greek from "Christian" tragedy. But the whole notion is in fact anachronistic. The modern reader slips into it easily because *we* think of two clear-cut alternative views—either we believe in free will or else we are determinists. But fifth-century Greeks did not think in these terms any more than Homer did: the debate about determinism is a creation of Hellenistic thought. Homeric heroes have their predetermined "portion of life" ($\mu o \hat{\iota} \rho a$); they must die on their "appointed day" ($a \check{\iota} \sigma \iota \mu o \nu \ \hat{\eta} \mu a \rho$); but it never occurs to the poet or his audience that this prevents them from being free agents. Nor did Sophocles intend that it should occur to readers of the *Oedipus Rex*. Neither in Homer nor in Sophocles does divine foreknowledge of certain events imply that all human actions are predetermined. If explicit confirmation of this is required, we have only to turn to lines 1230 f., where the Messenger emphatically distinguishes Oedipus' self-blinding as "voluntary" and "self-chosen" from the "involuntary" parricide and incest. Certain

[5] Sigmund Freud, *The Interpretation of Dreams* (London, Modern Library, 1938), 108.

of Oedipus' past actions were fate-bound; but everything that he does on the stage from first to last he does as a free agent.

Even in calling the parricide and the incest "fate-bound" I have perhaps implied more than the average Athenian of Sophocles' day would have recognized. As A. W. Gomme put it, "the gods know the future, but they do not order it: they know who will win the next Scotland and England football match, but that does not alter the fact that the victory will depend on the skill, the determination, the fitness of the players, and a little on luck." [6] That may not satisfy the analytical philosopher, but it seems to have satisfied the ordinary man at all periods. Bernard Knox aptly quotes the prophecy of Jesus to St. Peter, "Before the cock crow, thou shalt deny me thrice." The Evangelists clearly did not intend to imply that Peter's subsequent action was "fate-bound" in the sense that he could not have chosen otherwise; Peter fulfilled the prediction, but he did so by an act of free choice.[7]

In any case I cannot understand Sir Maurice Bowra's[8] idea that the gods *force* on Oedipus the knowledge of what he has done. They do nothing of the kind; on the contrary, what fascinates us is the spectacle of a man freely choosing, from the highest motives, a series of actions which lead to his own ruin. Oedipus might have left the plague to take its course; but pity for the sufferings of his people compelled him to consult Delphi. When Apollo's word came back, he might still have left the murder of Laius uninvestigated; but piety and justice required him to act. He need not have forced the truth from the reluctant Theban herdsman; but because he cannot rest content with a lie, he must tear away the last veil from the illusion in which he has lived so long. Teiresias, Jocasta, the herdsman, each in turn tries to stop him, but in vain: he must read the last riddle, the riddle of his own life. The immediate cause of Oedipus' ruin is not "Fate" or "the gods" —no oracle said that he must discover the truth—and still less does it lie in his own weakness; what causes his ruin is his own strength and courage, his loyalty to Thebes, and his loyalty to the truth. In all this we are to see him as a free agent: hence the suppression of the hereditary curse. And his self-mutilation and self-banishment are equally free acts of choice.

Why does Oedipus blind himself? He tells us the reason (1369 ff.): he has done it in order to cut himself off from all contact with humanity; if he could choke the channels of his other senses he would do so. Suicide would not serve his purpose: in the next world he would have to meet his dead parents. Oedipus mutilates himself because he can

---

[6] A. W. Gomme, *More Essays in Greek History and Literature* (Oxford, 1962), 211.
[7] B. M. W. Knox, *Oedipus at Thebes* (Yale, 1957), 39.
[8] C. M. Bowra, *Sophoclean Tragedy* (Oxford, 1944), ch. v.

face neither the living nor the dead. But why, if he is morally innocent? Once again, we must look at the play through Greek eyes. The doctrine that nothing matters except the agent's intention is a peculiarity of Christian and especially of post-Kantian thought. It is true that the Athenian law courts took account of intention: they distinguished as ours do between murder and accidental homicide or homicide committed in the course of self-defence. If Oedipus had been tried before an Athenian court he would have been acquitted—of murdering his father. But no human court could acquit him of pollution; for pollution inhered in the act itself, irrespective of motive. Of that burden Thebes could not acquit Oedipus, and least of all could its bearer acquit himself.

The nearest parallel to the situation of Oedipus is in the tale which Herodotus tells about Adrastus, son of Gordies. Adrastus was the involuntary slayer of his own brother, and then of Atys, the son of his benefactor Croesus; the latter act, like the killing of Laius, fulfilled an oracle. Croesus forgave Adrastus because the killing was unintended (ἀέκων), and because the oracle showed that it was the will of "some god." But Adrastus did not forgive himself: he committed suicide, "conscious" says Herodotus, "that of all men known to him he bore the heaviest burden of disaster." [9] It is for the same reason that Oedipus blinds himself. Morally innocent though he is and knows himself to be, the objective horror of his actions remains with him and he feels that he has no longer any place in human society. Is that simply archaic superstition? I think it is something more. Suppose a motorist runs down a man and kills him, I think he *ought* to feel that he has done a terrible thing, even if the accident is no fault of his: he has destroyed a human life, which nothing can restore. In the objective order it is acts that count, not intentions. A man who has violated that order may well feel a sense of guilt, however blameless his driving.

But my analogy is very imperfect, and even the case of Adrastus is not fully comparable. Oedipus is no ordinary homicide: he has committed the two crimes which above all others fill us with instinctive horror. Sophocles had not read Freud, but he knew how people *feel* about these things—better than some of his critics appear to do. And in the strongly patriarchal society of ancient Greece the revulsion would be even more intense than it is in our own. We have only to read Plato's prescription for the treatment to be given to parricides (*Laws* 872 c ff.). For this deed, he says, there can be no purification: the parricide shall be killed, his body shall be laid naked at a cross-

---

[9] Herodotus 1. 45. Cf. H. Funke, *Die sogenannte tragische Schuld* (Diss. Köln, 1963), 105 ff.

roads outside the city, each officer of the State shall cast a stone upon
it and curse it, and then the bloody remnant shall be flung outside the
city's territory and left unburied. In all this he is probably following
actual Greek practice. And if that is how Greek justice treated parricides, is it surprising that Oedipus treats himself as he does, when
the great king, "the first of men," the man whose intuitive genius had
saved Thebes, is suddenly revealed to himself as a thing so unclean
that "neither the earth can receive it, nor the holy rain nor the sun-
shine endure its presence" (1426)?

III

At this point I am brought back to the original question I asked the
undergraduates: does Sophocles in this play attempt to justify the ways
of God to man? If "to justify" means "to explain in terms of *human*
justice," the answer is surely "No." If human justice is the standard,
then, as Waldock bluntly expressed it, "Nothing can excuse the gods,
and Sophocles knew it perfectly well." Waldock does not, however,
suggest that the poet intended any attack on the gods. He goes on to
say that it is futile to look for any "message" or "meaning" in this
play: "there is no meaning," he tells us, "in the *Oedipus Rex*; there
is merely the terror of coincidence." [10] Kirkwood seems to take a rather
similar line: "Sophocles," he says, "has no theological pronouncements
to make and no points of criticism to score." [11] These opinions come
rather close to, if they do not actually involve, the view adopted by
my third and last group of undergraduates—the view that the gods
are merely agents in a traditional story which Sophocles, a "pure
artist," exploits for dramatic purposes without raising the religious
issue or drawing any moral whatever.

This account seems to me insufficient; but I have more sympathy
with it than I have with either of the other heresies. It reflects a
healthy reaction against the old moralizing school of critics; and the
text of the play appears at first sight to support it. It is a striking fact
that after the catastrophe no one on the stage says a word either in
justification of the gods or in criticism of them. Oedipus says "These
things were Apollo"—and that is all. If the poet has charged him with
a "message" about divine justice or injustice, he fails to deliver it.
And I fully agree that there is no reason at all why we should require
a dramatist—even a Greek dramatist—to be for ever running about
delivering banal "messages." It is true that when a Greek dramatic

[10] A. J. A. Waldock, *Sophocles the Dramatist* (Cambridge, 1951), 158, 168.
[11] G. M. Kirkwood, *A Study of Sophoclean Drama* (Ithaca, 1958), 271.

poet had something he passionately wanted to say to his fellow citizens he felt entitled to say it. Aeschylus in the *Oresteia,* Aristophanes in the *Frogs,* had something to say to their people and used the opportunity of saying it on the stage. But these are exceptional cases—both these works were produced at a time of grave crisis in public affairs— and even here the "message" appears to me to be incidental to the true function of the artist, which I should be disposed to define, with Dr. Johnson, as "the enlargement of our sensibility." It is unwise to generalize from special cases. (And, incidentally, I wish undergraduates would stop writing essays which begin with the words "This play *proves* that. . . ." Surely no work of art can ever "prove" anything: what value could there be in a "proof" whose premises are manufactured by the artist?)

Nevertheless, I cannot accept the view that the *Oedipus Rex* conveys *no* intelligible meaning and that Sophocles' plays tell us nothing of his opinions concerning the gods. Certainly it is always dangerous to use dramatic works as evidence of their author's opinions, and especially of their religious convictions: we can legitimately discuss religion *in* Shakespeare, but do we know anything at all about the religion *of* Shakespeare? Still, I think I should venture to assert two things about Sophocles' opinions:

First, he did not believe (or did not always believe) that the gods are in any human sense "just";

Secondly, he did always believe that the gods exist and that man should revere them.

The first of these propositions is supported not only by the implicit evidence of the *Oedipus Rex* but by the explicit evidence of another play which is generally thought to be close in date to it. The closing lines of the *Trachiniae* contain a denunciation in violent terms of divine injustice. No one answers it. I can only suppose that the poet had no answer to give.

For the second of my two propositions we have quite strong *external* evidence—which is important, since it is independent of our subjective impressions. We know that Sophocles held various priesthoods; that when the cult of Asclepius was introduced to Athens he acted as the god's host and wrote a hymn in his honour; and that he was himself worshipped as a "hero" after his death, which seems to imply that he accepted the religion of the State and was accepted by it. But the external evidence does not stand alone: it is strongly supported by at least one passage in the *Oedipus Rex.* The celebrated choral ode about the decline of prophecy and the threat to religion (lines 863–910) was of course suggested by the scene with Creon which precedes it; but it contains generalizations which have little apparent relevance either to Oedipus or to Creon. Is the piety of this ode purely conventional, as

Whitman maintained in a vigorous but sometimes perverse book? [12]
One phrase in particular seems to forbid this interpretation. If men
are to lose all respect for the gods, in that case, the Chorus asks,
τί δεῖ με χορεύειν; (895). If by this they mean merely "Why should I, a
Theban elder, dance?," the question is irrelevant and even slightly
ludicrous; the meaning is surely "Why should I, an Athenian citizen,
continue to serve in a chorus?" In speaking of themselves as a chorus
they step out of the play into the contemporary world, as Aristophanes'
choruses do in the *parabasis*. And in effect the question they are asking
seems to be this: "If Athens loses faith in religion, if the views of the
Enlightenment prevail, what significance is there in tragic drama,
which exists as part of the service of the gods?" To that question the
rapid decay of tragedy in the fourth century may be said to have
provided an answer.

In saying this, I am not suggesting with Ehrenberg that the character of Oedipus reflects that of Pericles,[13] or with Knox that he is
intended to be a symbol of Athens:[14] allegory of that sort seems to me
wholly alien to Greek tragedy. I am only claiming that at one point in
this play Sophocles took occasion to say to his fellow citizens something which he felt to be important. And it *was* important, particularly in the period of the Archidamian War, to which the *Oedipus
Rex* probably belongs. Delphi was known to be pro-Spartan: that is
why Euripides was given a free hand to criticize Apollo. But if Delphi
could not be trusted, the whole fabric of traditional belief was threatened with collapse. In our society religious faith is no longer tied up
with belief in prophecy; but for the ancient world, both pagan and
Christian, it was. And in the years of the Archidamian War belief in
prophecy was at a low ebb; Thucydides is our witness to that.

I take it, then, as reasonably certain that while Sophocles did not
pretend that the gods are in any human sense just he nevertheless held
that they are entitled to our worship. Are these two opinions incom-
patible? Here once more we cannot hope to understand Greek literature if we persist in looking at it through Christian spectacles. To the
Christian it is a necessary part of piety to believe that God is just. And
so it was to Plato and to the Stoics. But the older world saw no such
necessity. If you doubt this, take down the *Iliad* and read Achilles'
opinion of what divine justice amounts to (xxiv. 525–33); or take
down the Bible and read the Book of Job. Disbelief in divine justice
as measured by human yardsticks can perfectly well be associated with
deep religious feeling. "Men," said Heraclitus, "find some things unjust, other things just; but in the eyes of God all things are beautiful

[12] C. H. Whitman, *Sophocles* (Cambridge, Mass., 1951), 133–35.
[13] V. Ehrenberg, *Sophocles and Pericles* (Oxford, 1954), 141ff.
[14] B. M. W. Knox, op. cit., ch. ii.

and good and just." [15] I think that Sophocles would have agreed. For him, as for Heraclitus, there is an objective world-order which man must respect, but which he cannot hope fully to understand.

IV

Some readers of the *Oedipus Rex* have told me that they find its atmosphere stifling and oppressive: they miss the tragic exaltation that one gets from the *Antigone* or the *Prometheus Vinctus*. And I fear that what I have said here has done nothing to remove that feeling. Yet it is not a feeling which I share myself. Certainly the *Oedipus Rex* is a play about the blindness of man and the desperate insecurity of the human condition: in a sense every man must grope in the dark as Oedipus gropes, not knowing who he is or what he has to suffer; we all live in a world of appearance which hides from us who-knows-what dreadful reality. But surely the *Oedipus Rex* is also a play about human greatness. Oedipus is great, not in virtue of a great worldly position—for his worldly position is an illusion which will vanish like a dream—but in virtue of his inner strength: strength to pursue the truth at whatever personal cost, and strength to accept and endure it when found. "This horror is mine," he cries, "and none but I is *strong* enough to bear it" (1414). Oedipus is great because he accepts the responsibility for *all* his acts, including those which are objectively most horrible, though subjectively innocent.

To me personally Oedipus is a kind of symbol of the human intelligence which cannot rest until it has solved all the riddles—even the last riddle, to which the answer is that human happiness is built on an illusion. I do not know how far Sophocles intended that. But certainly in the last lines of the play (which I firmly believe to be genuine) he does generalize the case, does appear to suggest that in some sense Oedipus is every man and every man is potentially Oedipus. Freud felt this (he was not insensitive to poetry), but as we all know he understood it in a specific psychological sense. "Oedipus' fate," he says, "moves us only because it might have been our own, because the oracle laid upon us before birth the very curse which rested upon him. It may be that we were all destined to direct our first sexual impulses towards our mothers, and our first impulses of hatred and violence towards our fathers; our dreams convince us that we were." [16] Perhaps they do; but Freud did not ascribe his interpretation of the myth to Sophocles, and it is not the interpretation I have in mind. Is there not

[15] Heraclitus, fragm. 102.
[16] Sigmund Freud, op. cit., 109.

in the poet's view a much wider sense in which every man is Oedipus? If every man could tear away the last veils of illusion, if he could see human life as time and the gods see it, would he not see that against that tremendous background all the generations of men are as if they had not been, ἴσα καὶ τὸ μηδὲν ζώσας (1187)? That was how Odysseus saw it when he had conversed with Athena, the embodiment of divine wisdom. "In Ajax' condition," he says, "I recognize my own: I perceive that all men living are but appearance or unsubstantial shadow."

> ὁρῶ γὰρ ἡμᾶς οὐδὲν ὄντας ἄλλο πλὴν
> εἴδωλ᾽, ὅσοιπερ ζῶμεν, ἢ κούφην σκιάν.[17]

So far as I can judge, on this matter Sophocles' deepest feelings did not change. The same view of the human condition which is made explicit in his earliest extant play is implicit not only in the *Oedipus Rex* but in the *Oedipus Coloneus,* in the great speech where Oedipus draws the bitter conclusion from his life's experience and in the famous ode on old age.[18] Whether this vision of man's estate is true or false I do not know, but it ought to be comprehensible to a generation which relishes the plays of Samuel Beckett. I do not wish to describe it as a "message." But I find in it an enlargement of sensibility. And that is all I ask of any dramatist.

---

[17] *Ajax* 124–26.
[18] *O.C.* 607–15; 1211–49.

Drama in Sophocles' *Oedipus Tyrannus*

by E. T. Owen

I

The greatness of a Sophoclean tragedy is of course due, ultimately, to the greatness of the poet's mind, but this would have been of no avail if he had not devoted it singleheartedly to the business of his art. A great play must be first and foremost a great *play*, that is, it must be composed to do its work as such; the controlling purpose in its actual composition is the business of the play. What do I mean by the business of the play? I emphatically do not mean just getting the story told, making it work out according to necessity or probability, supplying motives for the action to lull to sleep our suspicions of its reality; I mean telling it so that one tense moment leads to another, so that the spectator's excitement is ever being aroused and satisfied simultaneously, held intent at every step and longing for the next, or, the same thing in a story, dreading it. This is the essence of drama-making, in any environment, by any means, for any purpose.[1]

"Drama in Sophocles' Oedipus Tyrannus*"* by E. T. Owen. *From* The University of Toronto Quarterly, X *(1940–41), 47–58. Copyright © 1940 by The University of Toronto Press. Reprinted in slightly abridged form by permission of the publisher.

[1] I append two brief statements, the first from the *Times Literary Supplement* (Feb. 18, 1926), the second from C. E. Montague's *Dramatic Values*, which emphasize essentials of drama often overlooked in more pretentious writings:

"When we ask what it is that drama can do better than anything else, we find that plot and character can be done nearly as well in most respects, and in point of fulness and detail much better, by the novel or other narrative forms of writing, but that the drama being a visible show is incomparable for crises, for those sudden turns of action which the eye takes in at a glance before a word is spoken, with the double advantage of a thrill for the audience and a saving of space for the dramatist. These critical moments are its moments of triumph, and a born dramatist so contrives his plot that a number of these follow one another in an ascending scale of excitement."

"Trained in the theatre, Ibsen knew precisely what a play was. He learned that a play has only one-tenth the length of a novel; that a play-goer, unlike a reader, cannot skip, and that therefore he must never be let fall into the state of mind in which, if he were reading, he would skip; he learned that dialogue is effective in a

If, then, we want to find out how the *Oedipus* creates the great impression it does, we should look for the explanation in the make-up of the play itself, not in an abstracted "idea of the drama." For proof of this one has only to read the many attempts to formulate its idea. However true they may be, they make it plain that what counts is not what the play means (in that sense) but what it is. Perhaps what I am trying to say is that the idea of the drama is the play itself, not something that can be extracted from it. It is just this combination of effects, through eye, ear, and mind, upon our emotions, and nothing else at all will express it. So in what follows I am not trying to sift out the idea of the play or get beyond it to Sophocles' mind or view of life, but simply noting how in a dramatic masterpiece the material has been handled to serve dramatic ends.

This may be only a first step, but it is vital as a starting point for further analysis. When we analyse, we should always keep in mind what the whole is which we are analysing. A play is and must be an arrangement of effects, and it is to its place in this whole that the dramatist, in composing, ultimately relates every scene and speech.

II

The groundwork of Sophocles' plan is to tell, through one action that begins and completes itself before our eyes without pause or rest, the story of Oedipus from his birth to his fall. He does this by making that action how Oedipus discovered the secret of his birth. His task therefore was to invent the circumstances of the discovery, and make it from start to finish an apparently inevitable process, a process that once begun constantly supplies its own reason for its continuance; for this is the condition that creates the feeling of tension, which is the basis of dramatic enjoyment. Thus his first objective, so far as the machinery of the plot is concerned, was to contrive the mutual confessions of Jocasta and Oedipus, and the scenes with Teiresias and Creon are, mechanically, the means for attaining it. Teiresias is provoked to denounce Oedipus as the slayer of Laius: Oedipus, concluding, from this outrageous charge, that there is a plot

---

theatre only when every speech produces a distinct change in the relations of the speakers, that it must carry the hearer over a rippled surface of small surprises to a foreseen goal, piquing curiosity in detail while meeting expectation on the whole. . . . When one of his characters speaks, you feel you really must hear the reply. When one of them comes upon the stage, you feel that for some minutes you have been coming to need his presence. . . . He plays on you like a flute, and knows every vent and stop of your attention. In a good play, your eye and ear together are kept in a state of expectancy constantly piqued and then satisfied, repiqued and resatisfied."

between the prophet and Creon to oust him from the throne, quarrels with Creon, and Jocasta appears to part them; her inquiry into the cause of the trouble leads to her inadvertent dropping of the first clue. Looked at just in this way the play might be judged slow in getting to work. Neither Teiresias nor Creon contributes anything directly to the telling of the story; they merely create the occasion for it. Two long scenes (running to over three hundred lines) are taken up with what looks like a single step in the advancement of the action, the bringing about of the scene between Oedipus and Jocasta. But while the story must be told, a dramatist's chief concern is not that, but to give the audience a good time by his way of telling it, to give them the best time he can, and this involves all sorts of considerations over and above getting the necessary facts of the story before them. Dramatic construction lies there.

We must bear in mind that Sophocles builds his effects on the audience's presumed knowledge of the outcome. He has therefore constructed these early scenes also to get the most out of the ironic contrast between appearance and reality. For there is here the opportunity not only of progressively sharpening and deepening the "irony," but of prolonging suspense, keeping the audience breathlessly waiting for the expected blow to fall. It is the plain duty of an alert artist to exploit these possibilities to the uttermost.

There are so many interests so closely intertwined that it is difficult to separate them for the purpose of analysis. The opening scene shows us a deputation of suppliants appealing to Oedipus for help against the plague: we see him as a grand figure towering godlike above the afflicted city, stooping down in gracious pity to share in and alleviate the sufferings of his subjects; but the background of this picture is our knowledge that he to whom they appeal is the cause of their plight, so that we are at the same time seeing him as a doomed man. One could almost say that all the dramatic elements in the situation are presented there in a kind of tableau, and the nature of our interest at once directed and keyed. The words spoken stress and point the moral of what the eye instantly takes in.

And then we hear that Oedipus has already sent Creon to the oracle at Delphi to find out the cause of the plague, and is impatiently expecting his return. Immediately there springs to mind the question, What will Apollo say? Apollo, of course, knows, Apollo whose original oracle stands, as it were, visibly before us translated into fact. Is it thus then that Oedipus is to hear the truth? Will Creon bring the dreadful tidings? So, when we hear that he is in sight, we wait, more excited than the stage auditors, for what he has to say. The moment passes, and we see our knowledge being moved, if anything, further away from Oedipus; we hear the story of Laius' slaying being wrongly told to Oedipus. (By "we" I here mean the original audience, who, though they knew the story of Oedipus, had no idea how Sophocles was going to unfold it.)

Then, after Oedipus' proclamation to the people of his resolve to search out the murderer of Laius in obedience to the oracle (which lengthy speech gives us time to review and savour the full irony of his position), the coming of Teiresias is announced—Teiresias whose name stands in story as synonymous with true prophecy. He must know surely; and as soon as he speaks, we know he does know. The truth is trembling on the brink of being told. But for those who know a secret there is a greater excitement than to see the ignorant just missing hearing it. You can bring the thing closer to them than that: by showing the ignorant actually hearing it in circumstances that cause them to disbelieve it, so that they hear it and miss hearing it at the same time; that is the height of this kind of excitement. We see in this scene our own knowledge put before the persons of the play, and, as we listen breathless, rejected. We have come as close to the revelation as it is possible to get, and yet it is still to be made. The scene is a triumph of dramatic understanding. The most important persons in a play are not the *dramatis personae* but the audience. Their needs are paramount, and the persons of the play are but instruments for satisfying those needs. Mahaffy says in criticism of the incident: "Teiresias tells him so explicitly that he is the murderer of Laius and the husband of his mother, that a man who knew his Corinthian parentage was doubtful, that an oracle had predicted to him this very crime, and that he had committed a homicide, could not but hit upon the truth." Perhaps a sufficient answer to this objection is that we do not know yet that Oedipus knows all these things, and while a psychological explanation of his blindness in the circumstances can be found if we stop to think it out, it is entirely unnecessary. I do not mean to suggest that Oedipus changes to fit the changing scenes; his blindness, besides being thrilling to observe in view of our knowledge, is indicative of his nature; and other interests of much deeper moment are being served by his behaviour towards Teiresias and Creon. Oedipus is being made to play a seemingly guilty part. We moderns do not instinctively take the point, which is perhaps the reason we falter rather over these two scenes, find them long drawn out and over-elaborated. But what is happening here is something that had a value for Sophocles' audience which it has not for us. For them it intensified the impression of coming doom. We, knowing to start with, as they did, that Oedipus is doomed, may feel no emotional value in these scenes save that of suspense, the holding back of the inevitable moment through Oedipus being delayed in his discovery by suspecting the wrong person, following up a false clue. But for the

Athenian spectators there was more in it than that; through these
scenes they were not just waiting for his doom to come, they were
seeing it coming, seeing him going to meet it, helping it along; for he
is behaving, or apparently behaving, as the man of ὕβρις [hubris]
proverbially behaves, and ὕβρις is in Greek story the certain precursor
of ruin. This is the general effect. At line 634 when Jocasta comes
between her husband and brother, Oedipus is on the verge of the
violent act which brings the hubristic man to disaster, and the play
marks the apparent crisis by raising the dialogue into music and sing-
ing as the chorus support Jocasta's plea by a solemn supplication to
their king to put away the evil spirit.

Of course it is not true; Oedipus is not guilty of ὕβρις. The dramatic problem is the opposite of that in *Macbeth*. "The interest in
the tragedy of Macbeth is the perpetration of crime by a man whose
magnificent qualities of mind, extreme courage, and poetic imagination raise the villainies above common meanness." [2] That is, the
Macbeth of the original story, being essentially guilty, must be raised
above his deeds, must be given some imaginative compensation to
win our sympathies; otherwise he will be just a bad man getting his
rich deserts, the spectacle of which, as Aristotle said, does not rouse
pity or fear. Oedipus is essentially innocent. What then must be done
with him? His innocence must be in some sort obscured; otherwise our
moral prepossessions will be aroused and flaw with their disquietudes
the emotional effect—not because Aristotle said it, but because it is so.
The shock must be softened. Modern readers do not instantly and
spontaneously seize the point, because the means used to attain the
effect is not for us immediately compelling; hence they go looking
for the moral alleviation in Oedipus' ἁμαρτία [hamartia], which they
find in one detail or another, especially in his hasty blow of retaliation
against an unprovoked assault. But if ἁμαρτία there is, that is not it.
The fact is, Oedipus' innocence is disguised, not really flawed. The
dramatist deliberately obscures the thought of his innocence; he
confuses his hearers' minds by setting them running on the familiar
ὕβρις theme, so that from association a false motivation of the calamity
is suggested, which gives it a seeming appropriateness, sufficient to
mitigate the immediate moral shock, but in the final effect, by the
contrast with the facts as otherwise shown, increasing enormously the
pathos and irony of his fate.

Some may question my assertion that Oedipus is represented as
essentially innocent. That is, they will say, to judge the situation
from a modern point of view; the Greeks would regard him as guilty
because with them guilt was in the deed, not the motive. But this

[2] "The Influence of the Audience on Shakespeare" (Robert Bridges, *Collected Essays*, 1927).

is a quibble; the Greeks could certainly distinguish between unwitting and deliberate guilt, and, if we could explain to them that we call unwitting guilt innocence, they would agree that, though they did not call it innocence, they thought about Oedipus just as we do. Our term is wider, but the feelings are the same.

Of the choral ode which separates the scenes with Teiresias and Creon, Jebb says:

> Teiresias has just denounced Oedipus. Why do not the chorus at once express their horror? This ode is the first since v. 215, and therefore in accordance with the conception of the chorus as personified reflection, it must comment on all that has been most stirring in the interval. Hence it has two leading themes: (1) "Who can be the murderer?": 1st strophe and antistrophe, referring to the first part of the preceding episode before the entrance of Teiresias. (2) "I will not believe that it is Oedipus": 2nd strophe and antistrophe referring to the second part.

It is difficult to speak with real confidence about the effect of the choral odes; with the best will in the world we cannot take them naturally, however much we may pretend to. What Jebb says about the orderly manner in which the chorus stick to their formal task may be quite right, but I question whether that is the sole justification. A choral ode, one would assume, depends for its effect on the knowledge possessed by the *audience*. They do understand what Teiresias has said, though the chorus do not, and therefore they have been seeing during this scene Oedipus' pursuing fate closing in upon him. Their sense of its significance is here put into words, but into such words as are in accordance with the knowledge of those that utter them. And as for the second half, while it is formally a comment on what Teiresias has said, is not its dramatic point, as Sheppard suggests, rather to call the attention of the audience to the fact that Oedipus' wisdom is undergoing now another test, and to throw up, by contrast of the chorus' steadfast loyalty to their tried ruler, Oedipus' ready suspicion of a tried friend? Creon's immediate entry on this note points the dramatic significance of the contrast.

The famous ode on the moral laws and the fate and character of the tyrant, which follows the first scene of the revelation (that with Jocasta) and precedes the catastrophe, may be considered most conveniently now. It is the central ode of the play, and is, from the point of view of choral tragedy, vital in its place. The chorus are, as Sheppard puts it, in a quandary: they believe in the oracles; they believe in Oedipus. They have now heard from Oedipus of the oracle that sent him wandering from Corinth; in the interests of their religious faith they must wish to see that oracle vindicated, and yet, according to tradition, such a calamity as it foretells can come only as a punishment of wickedness. They go over in their minds the traditional signs which prelude a great man's fall, and in the light of what they have seen and heard there is enough to make them afraid for Oedipus, afraid, that is, that he may have exhibited the fatal marks of ὕβρις. Thus the ode gathers up and establishes explicitly, as Greek tragedy has a habit of doing, the impressions conveyed by the action of the preceding scenes.

But it has finer and more truly dramatic merits than this; that is, it affects the mood in which the audience enter upon the next scene. The impressive opening strophe is constantly cited as if it were Sophocles' declaration of his own personal belief in the sanctities of the moral law, which of course it may as a matter of fact be, but to let it go at that is a tacit confession of inability to accept the choral odes as an integral part of the artistic structure. We should in any case assume that Sophocles wrote this ode to fit this particular place, and on that assumption I should say that its main function is to set the spiritual atmosphere which is to surround and colour the great event that follows. It puts into words, and hence crystallizes, the feeling aroused by the narratives of Jocasta and Oedipus, and by the intention and implications of those narratives—that is, the sense of moral chaos consequent upon the discrediting of the recognized means by which the gods make their will known to men. For the time being the moral laws seem abrogated, and it is in that atmosphere that the catastrophe takes place. But the catastrophe is in fact the triumph of the discredited oracles. Hence before the gloom and confusion in which the ode ends, which darken the stage for the horror of the disclosure, we are given a glimpse above the storm, as it were, of the sun still shining, of the eternal laws moving in serene majesty untouched by the darkness that envelops the earth. The storm that hides heaven from the sight of mortals is itself the means by which heaven will reveal its face again, and clear away the clouds that rose from earth. This does not necessarily represent Sophocles' judgment of the matter, but he wishes it for the moment to be felt like that, so that the catastrophe may be as effectively terrible and significant as possible while it occurs.

The central scenes contain the heart of the drama, that for which the rest exists—the drama of the revelation. The poet's task here is to make its effect adequate to the expectation. He manages to spin it out to nearly five hundred lines, and, instead of thinning, increases the excitement by spreading it out; it becomes a threefold revelation rising to a climax. We have here supreme dramatic skill in the way in which the incidents are manipulated. By the end of the first of these scenes Oedipus knows almost for certain that he is the slayer of Laius. The dramatist's next step therefore is to bring about the revelation that Laius is Oedipus' father. If we leave out Teiresias, as Sophocles does henceforth, nobody in the world of the play knows that. One fact known by one man (the Theban herdsman) must be added to another fact known by another (the Corinthian messenger) before it can be known. Sophocles has assured the coming of the first of these men through the one ray of hope in Oedipus' mind in regard to the identity of the man he killed. But since for the audience the effect of Oedipus' learning that he himself has slain Laius is fully enough attained in this scene, the dramatist brings in the Corinthian first, in order that the coming of the Theban herdsman may be the culmination of a new revelation, not a confirmation of the one whose effect we have already seen. By the time he arrives, Oedipus' interest has been switched to coincide with ours. It is the interest of the audience that determines the way the action is developed, and the motives and acts of the *dramatis personae* must be directed accordingly. So Sophocles interrupts the orderly progress of events by forcing in here the coming of the messenger from Corinth, the only accidental occurrence in the play. It is really a pure coincidence that he should arrive at just this juncture. But Sophocles deftly covers up its fortuitous nature by preceding it with Jocasta's prayer to Apollo to grant some clean way of deliverance from the trouble that seems to be gathering—a change in her attitude, natural enough, and effective in itself, but really aimed to pick up this little bit of dramatic value out of the necessary flaw. His coming looks on the face of it like an answer to her prayer—an ironical answer as of course we know it must be, but all the more dramatic for that. So it is one of those accidents which, as Aristotle says, do not seem to have happened quite by chance. And at once this effect is transformed into another dependent on it. Jocasta sees, in the news the Corinthian brings, release from all oracular fears. She forgets her prayer and feels no longer any need of Apollo's help. "Ye oracles of the gods, look where you are!" she cries mockingly and exultantly—a real dramatic thrill, for her cry calls sharp attention to the fact that with the messenger the oracles have arrived for their final confirmation. To that add also the thrill of horror that at such a moment she should blaspheme against the gods and, like Oedipus before her, by her own conduct make her own perdition sure.

Polybus' death, we realize, does in fact clear away an obstacle to the understanding of the oracle, but we see too that it must, on their present knowledge, remove for Oedipus and Jocasta its fulfilment from the bounds of possibility. Jocasta's words and attitude bring out the double point, express the effect we feel as an event occurring on the stage. No dramatic mind, contemplating the story of Oedipus, could overlook the opportunity of creating dramatic value by showing the oracle coming true through events that seem

to be disproving it. It is Jocasta's part to embody this interest, to
voice the conviction of the oracle's failure. That is the root of her
scepticism. Professor Goodell says: "Given an old myth to be dramatized, Sophocles' primary question was, 'Just what sort of people were
they, must they have been, who naturally did and suffered what the
tales say they did and suffered?' That was his method of analysis." I
do not think so, or at least it is not that kind of consideration which
gives these people their personalities. The situation of course calls
for certain figures in a certain relationship and there are certain
things they must do, and they must fit into their actions. But surely
it cannot be supposed that Sophocles thought out first, for example,
what Jocasta must have been like, and moulded his plot to accommodate that figure; rather he moulded his figure to accommodate his
plot, i.e., to accentuate dramatic possibilities he saw in the story.
Jocasta's scepticism about oracles is brought in not because in view
of her experience she would naturally or probably be sceptical, but
because it is dramatically valuable. Only those features in her, or any
other person's, probable character are used, which help to strengthen
and deepen the emotional effect of the whole.

In what mood Oedipus receives the news is not made perfectly
clear (Sophocles is a past master in knowing when not to explain);
the impression I get is that it is in the main one of unspeakable relief,
a relief that he is both ashamed to feel, because of the occasion, and
afraid to feel, lest there lurk in it some trick of fate. I think that
Sophocles deliberately obscures Oedipus' mood for a good dramatic
reason; he is making way for a difficulty. He wished to extract every
drop of dramatic effect that the situation could yield. The time for
the final revelation has come, and he has dared to prolong it, to make
it a double revelation, one to Jocasta, and another to Oedipus. Therefore he had to determine by what surge of feeling Oedipus is carried
unknowing past the point of Jocasta's enlightenment. For he must
not, and does not, represent him as merely incapable of putting two
and two together, as duller, less keen-witted than she. There is also
the difficulty of the divided interest between Jocasta and Oedipus—
how to get full value out of Jocasta's horror and yet to keep our attention on Oedipus. It must not be necessary for us to start up our interest
in Oedipus afresh after her departure. Two emotional currents must
be kept going simultaneously. I think this is managed with extraordinary skill. From that point in the dialogue which reveals the
truth to Jocasta, though we know what Oedipus is thinking, we do
not know what he is feeling, and we are longing to know. His short,
sharp questions show intense excitement, determined purpose, but no
more. The two interests—in Oedipus and Jocasta—come to a head
and clash in the dialogue between them, as he turns to her for informa-

tion—her wild desperate attempt to smother the truth away and his fierce determination to drag it into the light. Thus after Jocasta's terrible cry, which focuses the full horror of the situation, the scene does not drop; for we have been caught in the current of Oedipus' excitement, which rises to its climax and its explication in the glorious speech which ends the episode, and so on the crest of this we are swept forward towards the long-awaited catastrophe.[3]

In the course of this breath-taking scene the Corinthian has declared that he received the infant Oedipus from a shepherd belonging to the house of Laius, and the chorus-leader, appealed to by Oedipus, hazards the guess that this person is the very slave he has already summoned as the surviving eye-witness of Laius' slaying. "The *naïveté* of this guess," says Sheppard, "would be intolerable to a modern dramatist." If so, so much the worse for modern drama. The identification of the Corinthian's former acquaintance would in fact require more evidence, but the process of arriving at it would be tedious and blunt the effect. The first duty of drama is to be dramatic, not to reproduce the processes of actual life. Jocasta is the centre of interest at this particular moment, and Sophocles judges it right not to distract the attention from her. Of course, so far as this point goes, the chorus-leader need not have made any guess at all, but simply referred the question directly to Jocasta. But Sophocles is also preparing for the entrance of the herdsman; he wants us to know before he comes that he is the man who gave the child, in order that the present absorbing interest may run straight on, and not be interrupted by the business of recognition. For if we did not know, his entrance would be apparently carrying us back to an earlier interest that has now faded from our minds. As it is, the situation, when he enters, is masterly; each of the three actors is in a different state of expectation, as we know. We see them all, as they meet, on the edge of a great surprise. First, the Theban herdsman, expecting to be questioned about the slaying of Laius, and fencing cautiously, on that understanding, with the first inquiries of Oedipus, is instead suddenly confronted with a stranger and asked to identify him. Relieved and off his guard, he acknowledges the former meeting with him, and the Corinthian in his turn expecting to give the old man a pleasant surprise springs on him the identity of the baby he had then saved from death. All this is already known to Oedipus; there remains only the surprise for him, and it comes now

[3] "Break what break will!" (referring to the fear expressed by the chorus that evil will break from Jocasta's threat of future silence). "My origin, however lowly, I still shall wish to see. She perhaps, for she has proud thoughts for a woman, is ashamed of my base birth. But I, counting myself the child of Luck, the giver of good gifts, will not lose caste. I am that mother's son, and all my life the changing moons have seen me with them wax and wane. I could not now betray my nature and refuse to learn the truth about my birth."

swift and catastrophic. Steeled to accept, in the spirit of the child of Luck, alike what is bad and good in his present outlook, he is overwhelmed by the sudden flashing into complete and terrible coherence, of all the disjointed intimations of the past, showing that not chance but destiny has been leading him. This is quintessential drama. There has never been more perfect understanding of how to create true dramatic effect.

Oedipus Tyrannus

by Richmond Lattimore

The plot of *Oedipus,* beginning with the prologue and continuing through the next to the last episode, or act, concerns itself with the investigation of events which have already happened. It consists essentially in the joining together of pieces of information (*symbola* or "clues") until the last piece has been put in, the pattern completed, the puzzle solved. There are two principal problems: the detection of the murderer of Laius and the discovery of the identity of Oedipus himself; a manhunt combined with what might be called a rescue party. But both searches turn out to be after the same game, and the solution—discovery—is complete when the two are identified.

Thus, the drama belongs to the general story pattern of the lost one found. The lost one may be a lost husband, wife, brother, sister, or any close *philos,* thought dead far away but discovered to be present, unknown. A particularly popular variant has been the one that makes the lost one the lost baby or the foundling: the type to which *Oedipus* belongs. Whichever variant happens to be followed, the pattern of itself seems to generate certain features that are required, or almost required. For the foundling story, we may note the following: the child is noble; the child is unwanted and is put away (usually for destruction) and thought dead; but the method is always indirect (in Greek versions, a servant is usually delegated to do the dirty work) and the child is rescued, sometimes miraculously nursed by animals. The child grows up in the wilds, and is thought to be plebeian, but is at last recognized by infallible tests or unmistakable tokens and restored to its proper station. Thus the story is in part a story of the triumph of truth over rumor or opinion, and the triumph is pretty likely to come after the darkest moment, when error is on the point of prevailing.

A brief consideration of *Oedipus* will show that it follows the pattern almost perfectly. The tokens are not used by Sophocles toward the solution—he has another use for them—but they are there in the form of those otherwise so superfluously cruel pins stuck through the baby's ankles. It is also true that Oedipus is believed to be noble, though of the wrong noble stock: instead of being raised as the peasant's son, he is adopted by the great. In this, Oedipus resembles Ernest Moncrieff, alias Jack Worthing, in his black handbag deposited in the cloak room of Charing Cross Station. The resemblance is important. From the stories of Iamus, the young Cyrus, and Romulus, to the stories of Ernest and Ralph Rackstraw, the foundling story is a success story, a theme for what we call comedy or romantic comedy. But *Oedipus* is a true tragedy.

The tragically fulfilled story, mounted on so articulate a scheme for comedy, accounts for much of the essential nature of *Oedipus*. No extant tragedy so bristles with tragic irony. It opposes Oedipus—possessed of rumor, opinion, or, that is, error—against those who know —Tiresias, the Theban Shepherd—the latter two pulling back against revelation, because they know it is bad, as insistently as Oedipus, armed with his native wit (*gnōmē*) goes plunging forward. Where characters themselves are not omniscient, the audience is. They know the gist of the story and can be surprised only in the means by which the necessary ends are achieved. They know, for instance, that when Oedipus says (219–20):

> I shall speak, as a stranger to the whole question
> and stranger to the action

he is, in all sincerity, speaking falsehood, though the falsehood is qualified in the term stranger (*xenos*, outlander): the stranger who met and killed the king, the stranger who met and married the queen, who was no true stranger at all. Or when, at the outset, he says (59–61):

> For I know well
> that all of you are sick, but though you are sick, there's none
> of you who is so sick as I

he is, indeed, speaking the truth, but more truth than he knows, since he is using sickness metaphorically to describe the mental distress of a leader, himself sound, in a stricken kingdom. Oedipus keeps circling back on the truth and brushing against it, as if he subconsciously knew where it was; the omniscient audience can only wonder when the shock of contact will come.

In addition to this irony of detail, there is a larger irony in the inversion of the whole action. Tragic themes may mock the comic by matching them in reverse. Bassanio's three caskets are Lear's three daughters. Bassanio, marked for fortune, chooses the precious lead; Lear rejects it because he must suffer. The triumph of truth and virtue in the foundling play is the joyful recognition: "Our Perdita is found!" But to Oedipus, Tiresias says (449–54):

> I tell you: that man whom you have long been searching for
> with threats and proclamations for the murderer
> of Laius: that man is here.
> Supposed a stranger come to live with us, he shall
> be shown to be a genuine Theban, and will not
> be pleased with this solution.
>   Blind, who once saw clear,
> beggared, who once was rich, he shall feel out his way
> into a foreign country, with a stick.

The homeless wanderer by delivering the land from the monster and marrying the princess became prince in fact and then was shown to be prince by right, but this revelation turned him once more into a homeless wanderer. But the wanderer, who had once gone bright-eyed with his strong traveler's staff, now uses the staff to tap out the way before him, because he is now old, and eyeless.

The reversed pattern shows again in the fact that the malignant oracles have their darkest moment just before they come clear, with Jocasta's (946–47)

>   O prophesyings of the gods,
>   where are you now?

echoed and amplified in Oedipus' typical tyrant-speech of scepticism. Or consider the design of the helpers. The pattern story of the foundling requires a helper or rescuer: the merciful forester or herdsman who refuses to kill the baby outright, or who finds it and saves it from exposure (sometimes this is a wild animal). Sophocles provides at least one helper, or rescuer, for every act. The appeal in the prologue is to Oedipus, himself a rescuer (*sōtēr*) in the past; and Oedipus appeals to Creon, who comes from and represents Apollo and Delphi. It is as rescuer that Tiresias is called, Jocasta intervenes to help, so does the Corinthian Herdsman, and the last helper, the Theban Herdsman, is the true and original rescuer. Those who do not know are eager to help, those who know are reluctant, but all helpers alike push Oedipus over the edge into disaster. Again, it is the story as design which seems to dictate the actual ceremony of the blinding. The Greek word *arthron,* which means a socket, means also a piece which moves within a socket. The infant Oedipus was pinned through the ankles, the joints (*arthra*) of his feet, and while we would not speak of the joints of the eyes, *arthra* serves again for the eyeballs through which Oedipus sticks his wife's pins.[1] Thus the foundling-property of the pinned feet is ignored for its original purpose as means of recognition and transposed into a means of dramatic justice in Oedipus' self-vengeance, by which the strong man renders himself helpless as the baby was rendered helpless.

The fundamental story pattern demands precision in all detail where repeated words are positive, not suggestive, and nowhere else in tragedy is language so precise as here. Consider this piece in Jocasta's résumé (715–19):

> But Laius, so the report goes, was murdered
> by foreign brigands at a place where three roads meet.
> And for his son, only three days had passed since birth
> when Laius, pinning his feet together at the joints,
> gave him to other hands, and these abandoned him
> upon the mountain wilderness.

The lines are stiff with clues, which though they involve material facts (the three roads, the pinned feet, the mountain side), yet have holes in them (the reported brigands, the second-hand casting away), and they are arranged so that the clue of the three roads forces Oedipus to fix on the fight with the king, and ignore the still more glaring clue that should lead to his own identification with the castaway baby.

The plausibility of this, if it stands, is a case of the probable-impossible, or drama more perfect than actual life. The pattern story demands tailoring; and if this were a true report of real action, we could ask some awkward questions. For example: Why did the servant of Laius (Theban Shepherd) give the false report of *a body of brigands?* Why did he say nothing when he saw Oedipus in Thebes, but ask to go to the country? Why was he treated so well, when he had run away and left his master and fellow-servants dead on the road? One may answer these: he suspected the truth all the time, beginning with the encounter on the road, for he knew that the son of Laius had not died, and recognized him in this young man who looked like Laius,[2] he was loyal to his protégé, and perhaps disliked Laius, of whom no good has ever been told, here or elsewhere; the story of a body of brigands protected both him and Oedipus. These answers are plausible, but are we intended to work them out, or is there even time to consider them in the rapid progress of the action? This is not the tragedy of the Theban Shepherd. He is an agent, not a principal.

---

[1] See Liddell and Scott [*A Greek-English Lexicon*], s.v. ἄρθρον. For the pinned feet, see lines 718, 1032, 1349; see also Euripides' *The Phoenician Women* 804–5: Οἰδιπόδαν. . . . χρυσοδέτοις περόναις ἐπίσαμον; also frg. 557, Nauck (from the *Oedipus* of Euripides). For golden pins to fasten the (foundling) child Dionysus, see Euripides *The Bacchae* 97–98. For the pins through the eyes, see our text, 1268–79.

[2] Line 743.

There are other points of verisimilitude it would be possible but tedious to raise.[3]

But Sophocles himself raised a couple of questions which he did not answer. Why, if Tiresias was wise and inspired, positively omniscient, did *he* not answer the Sphinx?[4] Why, after the death of Laius and arrival of Oedipus, did he say nothing about the connection?[5] Creon's answer to this last is sage and temperate (569):

> I do not know. And where I have no idea I prefer
> to keep quiet.

But it does not take us far. Is it not, rather, that Oedipus is the man who must find, and condemn, and punish himself? As for the question, why did Tiresias not answer the Sphinx? Grant that it was awkward of Sophocles to raise this, or the other question, when he would not, or could not, answer. In this second case, the Sphinx is one of those barbarous primeval figures who haunt the edges of tragedy. An amorous[6] she-fiend who asks childish riddles and destroys those who cannot answer serves with effect as a vaguely indicated background bogey, or as a blazon on a shield by Aeschylus,[7] but scrutinized close-up she must turn ludicrous; so, in the tetralogy of Aeschylus, she draws the satyr-play.[8] But if the question *were* answered: again, it was not for Tiresias to solve this. As Perdita is lost, so she can be found; so the Sphinx is there for Oedipus to answer. To say he was "fated" to is to overstate it with prejudice toward the grand designs of heaven; but it is a part of his pattern or story-*tychē*, which in Greek does not mean "fate," "chance," or "fortune" so strictly as it means "contact,"[9] or, say, "coincidence," the way things are put together.

The pieces fit. The missing one who has been hunted is found. This is the special sense sometimes implicated in the cry *iou iou,* the cry which Oedipus and Jocasta, and Heracles in *The Women of Trachis,* give when the truth is out,[10] the hunter's cry of Socrates in the *Re-*

---

[8] For instance, why had Oedipus never gone even superficially into the question of the murder? Some awkwardness is felt and shown in lines 105–31. Or again, how could Jocasta know *nothing* (lines 774–75, often and justly admired) about the stranger she married?

[4] Lines 390–400.

[5] Lines 558–68.

[6] On sphinxes and sirens, both subsumed as types of *kēr,* see Harrison, *Prolegomena,* pp. 197–212; on the amorous sphinx, see J. Ilberg, in Roscher's *Lexikon,* IV, s.v. "Sphinx," esp. cols. 1381–85; in general, see Robert, *Oidipus,* pp. 48–50.

[7] *The Seven* 539–43.

[8] Argument to Aeschylus, *The Seven.*

[9] So at least I should judge, with perhaps insufficient authority, by simply combining the senses of τυγχάνω- "hit" with τεύχω- "make."

[10] Jocasta, line 1071; Oedipus, line 1182; Heracles, in *The Women of Trachis* 1143.

public when the quarry for which he and his friends have beaten far bushes is seen to be grovelling right at their feet.[11]

But after discovery, Oedipus does one more thing to complete the pattern. He blinds himself, as reported in the one true messenger-scene of the drama, from the anonymous Messenger who gives us, not the fact of the ruin of Oedipus, for we knew that already, but only the cruel ceremonies through which that ruin is displayed (1251–79):

> And how she perished after that I do not know,
> for Oedipus burst in, shouting aloud, and made
> it impossible to watch the rest of her agony
> because our eyes were on him as he stalked the court
> and ranged among us, crying to be given a sword,
> crying to find that wife who was no wife, that field
> that bore a double crop, himself and his children.
> As the man raved, it was some spirit showed him.
> It was not any man of us who stood close by.
> With a fierce cry, as if something were guiding him,
> he drove against the double doors, and from their bases
> buckled the panels inward and burst into the room.
> There we looked in, and saw the woman hanging, caught
> in a noose of rope. But he
> when he looked at her, moaning horribly, he loosed
> the knot from her throat. Then, when the poor woman was laid
> upon the ground, the rest was terrible to see.
> Tearing the golden pins by which her dress was clasped
> out of the robes she wore
> he raised them, stabbed them into the balls of both his eyes,
> crying that they should never more look on himself,
> nor on the evils done to him, or what he had done,
> but that their sight of those they should not look upon
> must darken, lest they recognize whom they should not.
> To such an incantation, many times, not once,
> he dashed the pins into his eyes, and from the eyeballs
> the blood ran down his chin, nor was the storm an ooze
> and drip, but there came both
> a dark clear rain and clotted hail, and all was blood.[12]

What was the sword for? The question is left flying in the air as Oedipus sees Jocasta, already dead. But why does Oedipus blind himself? Students of motivation will find their answer. So that the eyes should no longer look upon the people, the things, that they

[11] Plato's *Republic* iv. 432D.

[12] The text is uncertain here, and I do not try to give more than the general sense, which seems to combine blood (dark but clear) and fragments of matter (not clear, also bloody), the rain and hail respectively.

should not. Sophocles says so. He repeats it: how could Oedipus share
sensibilities with his fellow citizens, with whom he can now share
nothing? If he could have shut off the sources of hearing, he would
have:[13] thus making himself, we might add, the outcast who was to be
banned from the community,[14] because the murderer was to be that
outcast, and Oedipus is the murderer. We add this; but Sophocles adds
that it would be sweet for Oedipus to cut himself loose from all evils,
from all his life he knows now as evil; and then seems to contradict
himself when Oedipus cries for his daughters and calls them into his
arms.[15] But by then, the mood of frenzy has ebbed along with the
strength of fury, and Oedipus is himself again, reasoning, and justifying.

Then, for the wildness of Oedipus when he stabbed his eyes, could
we say that reasoning of any kind is too reasonable? At least we can
say that Oedipus' self-blinding can be seen from various angles. It
seems to be a punishment of what is evil (*kakon*), for Oedipus does
not deign to call himself *kakodaimōn,* unlucky, ill-starred, but just
evil (or vile), *kakos.*[16] The evil Jocasta has escaped; the fury turns on
himself with, as we have seen, the formal mode of transfixing those
socketed balls of his eyes.

But blinding still serves one more purpose. The riddle of the
Sphinx spoke of man feeble as a baby, man strong as grown man
(walking on two feet), man feeble in old age. And we have had Oedipus as baby, and Oedipus as grown man, a strong traveler walking
on his two feet.[17] We need Oedipus old and enfeebled, and he is still
a man in his prime, and appallingly strong. Only such a catastrophic
self-punishment can break him so that, within moments, he has turned
into an old man, who (1292)

> needs strength now, and needs someone to lead him.

So he has lived the three stages. The riddle of the Sphinx was the
mystery of man. But it was the specially private mystery of Oedipus.
This—the Sphinx might have meant to him—is the mystery of you.
Solve it. *Gnōthi sauton.*

In this sense, but I think in this sense only, Oedipus is Everyman.
Stories such as these have shapes of their own which force action
rather than shapes which are forced by reason or character; and hence,

---

[13] Lines 1384–90.
[14] Lines 233–51.
[15] Lines 1480–81.
[16] The word *kakos* is used many times in this play, but the most interesting ap-
plications of it may be found at lines 76, 822, 1063, 1397, 1421.
[17] Line 798.

romantic comedy tends to refine plot at the expense of personality, with stock or pattern situations generating stock characters.[18] But this does not have to happen. Eteocles in *The Seven* is also bent by the shape of the story but generates a momentum which makes his necessary act his own. So is Oedipus. He is the tragedy tyrant driven by his plot, but he is more, a unique individual and, somehow, a great man, who drives himself.

[18] On these matters in general, see Kitto, *Greek Tragedy*, pp. 270–71.

Oedipus Tyrannus: Appearance and Truth

by Karl Reinhardt

The tension of this drama has been much noticed. What sustains it is by no means simply the breathless, inexorable advance of a discovery getting under way. Nor is it merely a matter of hidden fate playing cat and mouse with an unsuspecting victim,[1] or of an interplay of misconceptions intruding into an inquiry, in the course of an investigation—in a word, not the stuff of so many dramas of discovery written since. Schiller, in a phrase which those after him have cited far too often, dubbed the *Oedipus* a "tragic analysis." "Everything is present in it already," he said. "It is merely brought into the open. . . . Moreover, since the events are unalterable, they are intrinsically much more frightful. . . ." (to Goethe, October 2, 1797). In saying this he was concentrating far too much on the pragmatic arrangement and far too little on the essence, a reflection of his own work on *Wallenstein.* For Sophocles, as for Greeks of an earlier period, fate is, generally speaking, never deterministic, but is instead a spontaneous revelation of the power of the demonic. This is equally true when it has been foretold, and true even when it is brought about through an order immanent in events and their cosmic movement. A deterministic fate is not to be found before the Stoa and the triumph of astrology.[2] In the *Oedipus,* too, what is essential is not an immutable

---

"Oedipus Tyrannus: *Appearance and Truth*" (editor's title) by Karl Reinhardt. From Sophokles, 3rd ed. (Frankfurt am Main: Vittorio Klostermann, 1947), pp. 107–14, 143–44, 268–69, 273–74. Copyright 1947 by Vittorio Klostermann. Translated into English, with permission of the publisher, by Michael J. O'Brien. The translator is grateful to Mr. Ingolf Grape, who read an early draft of this version and made valuable suggestions.

[1] So, e.g., Volkelt, *Ästhetik des Tragischen* (1906), p. 417: "In *Oedipus the King* particularly, fate obtrudes its presence upon us as a process of entrapment which moves towards its goal despite all attempts to evade it, as a spiteful, subtle arrangement of circumstances which plunges to inevitable destruction that man against whom the god has designs." In this statement, only the external, factual arrangement is taken into account: the whole spiritual struggle of the first part is left out of consideration.

[2] Wilamowitz is almost alone in opposing the acceptance of the notion "tragedy of fate," in his Introduction to the translation of the *Oedipus,* p. 11 ff. However, the distinctions that he makes are different.

past in process of disclosing itself—there is no place in the *Oedipus* for Schiller's "Can it be? Can I no longer do as I would?"—but rather a battle, actively waged, for deliverance, for self-assertion, and for the defense of a whole structure of appearance, proper to man and indeed intimately bound up with his greatness, which is under attack. This structure must, for its own order, "truth," and stability, reverse the distinctions between appearance and being. In contrast to other Greek tragedies, the *Oedipus* is not at all, as one might think, the tragedy of human fate (though it has long been regarded as the archetype of such tragedy), in which "fate," in accordance with the views of German classical thought, was always to be set against "freedom" —indeed "sublime freedom." [3] Better to call it, in contrast to other Greek tragedies, the tragedy of appearance in human life, in which the correlative of appearance is being, as in Parmenides Aletheia [Truth] is of Doxa [Opinion]. It might indeed have been noticed that of all its choral odes not one sings of fate, a common enough subject elsewhere, but that one ode, in a prominent place, sings of human "appearance" (line 1189):

> For who among men, who
> seizes more of happiness
> than the appearance of it, only to fall
> when that appearance has scarcely been won?

The defensive battle conducted from the ground of appearance begins imperceptibly, but is already under way with the opening of the divinely ordained inquiry. It starts with a curious change in the direction of that inquiry, a deviation which Voltaire, speaking as a logician, properly took notice of but then improperly criticized.[4] After an investigation of the facts of the case seems already to have been planned, after the question has already been put, "Is there a witness?" and after this has been answered in the affirmative (line 118), a sudden suspicion attaches itself to the word "robber," one which upsets the intention of the inquiry. How could robbers have run such a risk unless bribed "from here"? "From here": that is to say, from somewhere in Thebes. The question, which bears on a king's murder and is posed by a king himself, is readily understood. The question points to Creon. Creon gives the appearance of evading it: the suspicion, he says, that unavoidably arose could not be pursued after the deed. Why not? The Sphinx came. . . . For some time after this, to be sure, the suspicion seems to lie dormant. But the focus of attention is no longer on the scene of the crime, or the way it hap-

---

[3] "Fate" in opposition to "man's moral freedom," e.g., in A. W. Schlegel, *Vorles. über dram. Kunst*, p. 178, p. 204, and elsewhere.
[4] *Lettre III sur Oedipe*; cf. Bruhn's commentary (1910), p. 25.

pened, or the instrument, but rather on those ultimately responsible, and Thebes. Then suddenly, after the quarrel with the hostile and apparently malevolent prophet, the suspicion is confirmed, the connection between Creon and Teiresias is established, and the existence of a whole web of enmity stands corroborated as fact.

As it happens, the only fragment still preserved from the *Oedipus* of Aeschylus is one in which a witness, evidently the sole survivor, tells us of the "crossroads." The discovery, or a part of the discovery, must of necessity have followed after this point. Nowhere in Sophocles' whole drama is an inquiry of this sort to be found. The Aeschylean fragment lets us see precisely what it was that Sophocles thrust aside, by means of that deviation and its wider consequences, in order to make room for something else.

For because of it the original appearance, which was unavoidable and (one might say) inborn, is joined by a new appearance in the form of a delusion. Moreover, the way in which this new appearance makes its entry—as a suspicion of bribery, of a secret plot in the midst of the city which was its intended target—reveals the influence in the *Oedipus* of that dramatic and scenic form, that external vesture under which appearance had made itself Creon's master in the *Antigone*.[5] In that play, the suspicion of a bribe, at first merely intimated in the word κέρδος [profit] (line 222), and then overshadowed by intervening material, suddenly appeared fully formed and destined to be enlarged in the prophet-scene (line 290 ff.). So it is in the *Oedipus Tyrannus* as well. In the *Antigone*, however, the suspicion had already been suggested to the new ruler by the external situation as he found it: the heir to the throne had just died, the exile had just been overthrown. . . . The suspicion was already hidden in the first edict, the prohibition against burying the enemy of the land. In the *Oedipus*, the ruler steps before the community as an object of everyone's respect, surrounded and addressed with fervent invocations, unlike Creon, who announces his own entrance. Therefore, the menace hardly seems grounded in the external situation. Nevertheless, a similar suspicion hovers over this scene too, one which remains without a specific object until the moment it hurls itself, by way of Teiresias, against Creon. In other words, the menace in the *Oedipus* enters more into the humanly subjective sphere, penetrates further into the region of the spirit; it is scented and intuited from the demonic elusiveness of the problem rather than deduced from external circumstances. And the false fixation has its source in the need of a man who is the captive of appearance to have an enemy that he can grasp, in order that he may not lose his security. In Creon's case, a

[5] On the similarity of the two scenes, see Bruhn in his commentary, p. 33 ff. (where, however, the chronological inferences are incorrect).

violation of the ban would have posed in itself no threat to his existence. For Oedipus everything is at stake, even before he suspects what he has at stake: his world of appearance, which finds itself threatened, not at first however by truth, but by the illusory product of its own making (line 137):

> *Oedipus.* For not on behalf of distant friends,
> but on my own behalf do I remove this infamy.
> For whoever struck him dead—how easily
> might he move with like hand against me!

The irruption of the truth—here one ought not to speak of "reality," since Oedipus at first lives not in illusion but in objective falsity and mere semblance—the irruption, to repeat, of the truth into the structure of appearance is a result of successive incursions at two points, the first on its periphery, the second at its center; first, through the question, "What is the thing hidden there before me, which it is my function to bring to light?" and then through the other question, "What am I, and what is my own proper being?" At first the latter question remains hidden behind the former, then for some distance they move side by side in secret concert, only to merge in the end. At all times the structure seeks to maintain itself, and it hurls its forces against the point from which the threat comes.

The defense against the still unknown enemy begins with the sentence of outlawry, and with it the curse. Oedipus knows how to curse, and his authority lends strength to his curse. As soon as the act of cursing takes hold of him, he proclaims those words which entail their own fulfillment, which are public and at the same time personal; he curses with priestly dedication and, as it were, with ruffled plumage. . . . When one considers Euripidean curses, e.g. the one spoken by Theseus in the *Hippolytus,* it becomes clear how little affinity Euripides has for this type of language and what it expresses. But one's disappointment is perhaps even greater if one compares the fragment, by chance preserved, of the old epic, the *Thebaid* (frag. 3), where not a word of the curse finds its way into the poetic description. We find the statement, "He cursed" . . . and nothing further.

The power of the curse-speech is all the greater for being clearly directed against the speaker himself without his knowledge. Creon's oaths in the *Antigone* were also directed against the speaker; but how much more fateful is the power with which the curse is turned back upon Oedipus in this play! Like Creon's speeches in the *Antigone,* this curse too has its own dynamic of mounting intensity. Once more, after a gentle beginning, agitation sets in; in it one recognizes the demeanor of a man in danger of sinking into delusion. Once more too a reversal takes place between the first part and the last, although in the *Oedipus* it is not achieved through dialogue, but merely through the evolving movement of the speech of malediction itself. The moderate tone with which the speaker began, promising impunity to the criminal if he should confess, is lost once the solemn act of outlawry has been decreed. The very force of the curse and condemnation takes possession of the speaker as the riddle that he wants to solve draws him more and more to itself:

> So will I fight on the god's side,
> and on the side of the slain man!
> But my curse be on the one who did this, whether he is alone
> or conceals his share in it with others.
> Let him be free of no misery till his last day!
> And a like curse on myself if he share my house
> or sit at my hearth and I have knowledge of it.
> On myself may it fall, as I have called it down on him!

Detachment marks the new king's first reaction to the unknown, virtually forgotten event; but later there develops in him a strangely growing intimacy with these alien concerns, as if they were his own. Without suspecting the connection, he is already making himself his father's son; in the demonic sphere of appearance he is already grasping, magically and proleptically, his own true being. Detachment marks the beginning of the speech (line 219):

> So do I proclaim, although to such report I am a stranger
> and to the thing itself, for otherwise I should not need
> to track from so far off, and without a clue.
> But now, since late did I first win rights
> in your city, I proclaim to all you
> Cadmeans: . . .

It is still the same detachment as before (line 103):

> *Creon.* Laius, my lord, was of this land
>   the king, before you stood at the helm.
> *Oedipus.* I heard of him, yet saw him not.

But the detachment is transformed into an ever stronger participation (line 258):

> . . . But now, since I
> hold the sovereign authority which was his,
> share the couch that was his, share his wife
> with him equally for conception of seed,
> indeed had shared children of the same womb too
> had not a misfortune struck his race—
> but, as it happened, his destiny fell upon him:

therefore will I, as if he were my own father,
fight on his behalf until the very end,
until I reach the man guilty of the blood
of the son of Labdacus, son of Polydorus,
son of old Cadmus, son of ancient Agenor.[6]

There at the end stands the full lineage, reckoned up—as when a man speaks for his whole line. So it is that kings name their ancestors one after the other when they swear oaths, like Xerxes in Herodotus (VII, 11): "May I not be thought the son of Darius, son of Hystaspes, son of Arsames, son of Ariaramnes, son of Theispes, son of Cyrus, should I not take my revenge on the Athenians." [7]

The apparent detachment and the apparent appropriation of what is not his own (for the true act of appropriation takes place only through his downfall) are, both of them, it is true, tragic-ironic. But it is not until this act of appropriation, even at the moment when it is only apparent, and the passionate vehemence with which it leaves behind all that depends on mere facts, that being and appearance are irreparably intertwined and interwoven one with the other. It is in this tight bond, no longer external or pragmatic, but demonic, enclosing his whole being, his very soul, the very language he uses, that there first emerges the tragedy of the man expelled from his world of appearance. We have here as well the answer to the question: What would Oedipus be to us if he did not happen to be Laius' son? or How does the symbolic form of the drama find a source in the unique details of the legend? The demonic, incessant, and blind reaching across boundaries, from the realm of appearance into the realm of truth, is the universally human aspect—not present in the·legend— which was first associated with the figure of Oedipus because of Sophocles.[8] At the same time, it is this which constitutes that ironic quality which is usually labelled and generalized, in accordance with an academic conception of our aesthetic theory, as "tragic irony." The phrase is quite inexact, for the point is not that the spectator's own knowledge surpasses that of Oedipus as he gropes in darkness, so that the latter's words have a different ring for him. It is rather that man-

---

[6] In the translation of Wilamowitz the period, in which the anacoluthon is evidence of the inner movement, is split into two parts, inasmuch as the νῦν δὲ of line 263 is referred back to the νῦν δὲ of line 258 and a full stop is placed after ἡ τύχη in line 263.

[7] Hofmannsthal, in *Oedipus and the Sphinx*, has fashioned whole scenes (with rather fine effect) out of the way in which Oedipus strays, without suspecting it, into his own domain and the heritage of his own blood. In Sophocles this takes place through the tone and movement of the speech.

[8] Tycho von Wilamowitz-Moellendorf, *Dram. Technik*, p. 86, would disagree: "It is evident that Oedipus' delusion is always required by the plot" etc. Similarly E. Howald [*Die Griech. Tragödie* (1930) (*Editor's note*)], p. 111.

kind is shown entangled in appearance and being, and appearance and being are not merely apportioned or exchanged between stage and auditorium—let alone between a poet as subject and his poetic world—but rather they encounter each other in every word, every gesture of the one who errs. It is not the poet who carries on this game with human appearances, through the medium of his own theatrical world of appearance, but the invisible gods, from a background which is beyond our grasp.

After the secret, unrecognized, ominous battle is over, the open battle between truth and appearance begins, in the Teiresias-scene. The battle is not in this case between truth and error. For when one speaks of "error" one does not mean an inevitable failure, such as we have here, a flaw not of the mind but of the whole human condition, both internal and external. Deianira in the *Trachiniae* found herself in tragic error. Something burst upon her which caused her remorse as soon as she grasped it. In the same play Heracles raged in tragic error. . . . Tragic error is something that overtakes man. But tragic appearance, in which Oedipus finds himself, and which undoubtedly is typical of tragic art in its more profound form, is something that encloses and conditions man from the beginning—that is to say, what he is and what he wills to be, king, husband, leader, savior; it is his strength and security; it is everything that keeps him safe. The Creon of the *Antigone* was driven into what was false and merely apparent; Oedipus stands within the realm of appearance and is hurled out of it.

*   *   *

Yet in this act of revelation one question is not brought up which later ages (one sees this already in Euripides) seem unable to dissociate from tragedy: Where does the blame lie? Oedipus certainly does speak of himself in terms used of a criminal, as one guilty of another's death.[9] But that still does not raise the question of blame ($a\dot{\imath}\tau\dot{\iota}a$). The god is, to be sure, named as the author, but not in order that man may prevail over god or prevail over himself in the sight of god, nor in order that he may wrestle with god or destroy himself before god for his fault, but rather to indicate the correlation of man and god. The reference to god is also part of the revelation: the manifestation of the divine coincides with the manifestation of the human:

> *Oedipus.* Apollo, it was Apollo, friends,
>   who brought about this pain for me, my pain.
>   But the bloody hand that struck me was
>   none other than my own, wretch that I am! [10]

---

[9] $\mathring{a}\theta\epsilon os$, $\mathring{a}\nu o\sigma\acute{\iota}\omega\nu$ $\pi a\hat{\iota}s$, $\mathring{a}\sigma\epsilon\beta\acute{\eta}s$ etc.

[10] The words that bear the main stress are "Apollo" and "I"; the two actions coincide, correspond, or imply each other. If one is willing to construe the arrange-

Even the language of sacred law, which rings clearly here, can in no way alter this omission. It is rather that this language is used because sacred law is concerned with the same basic principles and rules of life that are at issue here. Yet there is no question of a "guilty party" in the sense associated with sacred law either. A court of gods or of men, it might be supposed, would acquit Oedipus of all blame, like the Aeschylean Orestes; yet this would still be of no help to him, for what would such an acquittal be worth, set against the contradiction between what he supposed himself to be and what he is? And conversely, a verdict of "guilty" would not make things worse for him. Orestes *can* be acquitted by himself and by others, but Oedipus *cannot* escape what he has learned about himself. The question of responsibility for what happened, wherever and however it might have been asked, whether this responsibility was to be borne by men, by the gods, or by the world-order, and whether the question was to be answered with a yes or a no—the question, without which the greatest tragic art of Euripides and Aeschylus is unthinkable, is left out. So nothing is decided here about justice and atonement (it would be utterly absurd to let the blinding stand as an atonement), and nothing about freedom and necessity either,[11] but much about appearance and truth as the opposites between which man is bound, and by which he is ensnared, and in whose chains, as he reaches towards the heights of his aspiration, he consumes and shatters himself.

---

ment of the two sentences with a close enough logic, one can interpret it to mean: "Apollo (as the spiritual author, so to speak) planned it and brought it to its goal; I carried it out," although τελῶν, to judge from its position, does not stand in such a strong antithetical relation. Besides, it all simply comes to the same thing; for in any case the distinction, considering the weight of "I," could still never be interpreted in such a way as to exculpate the agent or distinguish the human and divine design and execution from one another, thereby allotting man his share of blame (as in the translation of Wilamowitz). The whole thing is an answer to the question, "What kind of daemon drove you?" There is no doubt that a god is active in deeds of this kind.

[11] So Pohlenz, inasmuch as he regards freedom of "action" as preserved in spite of all, *Griech. Tragödie,* p. 224: "And however shocking the external appearance of the blinded man may appear to us, there lies in his free act, in the way he faces his destiny, a greatness which can exalt us." This is in the tradition of Schiller.

Oedipus: Ritual and Play

by Francis Fergusson

The Cambridge School of Classical Anthropologists has shown in great detail that the form of Greek tragedy follows the form of a very ancient ritual, that of the *Eniautos-Daimon,* or seasonal god.[1] This was one of the most influential discoveries of the last few generations, and it gives us new insights into *Oedipus* which I think are not yet completely explored. The clue to Sophocles' dramatizing of the myth of Oedipus is to be found in this ancient ritual, which had a similar form and meaning—that is, it also moved in the "tragic rhythm." [2]

Experts in classical anthropology, like experts in other fields, dispute innumerable questions of fact and of interpretation which the layman can only pass over in respectful silence. One of the thornier questions seems to be whether myth or ritual came first. Is the ancient ceremony merely an enactment of the Ur-Myth of the year-god—Attis, or Adonis, or Osiris, or the "Fisher-King"—in any case that Hero-King-Father-High-Priest who fights with his rival, is slain and dismembered, then rises anew with the spring season? Or did the innumerable myths of this kind arise to "explain" a ritual which was perhaps mimed or danced or sung to celebrate the annual change of season?

For the purpose of understanding the form and meaning of *Oedipus,* it is not necessary to worry about the answer to this question of

---

[1] See especially Jane Ellen Harrison's *Ancient Art and Ritual,* and her *Themis* which contains an "Excursus on the ritual forms preserved in Greek Tragedy" by Professor Gilbert Murray.

[2] In an earlier passage in his book (p. 18), Fergusson has explained "tragic rhythm" as the movement which constitutes the shape of the whole play and of each episode in the play. He adds: "Mr. Kenneth Burke has studied the tragic rhythm in his *Philosophy of Literary Form,* and also in *A Grammar of Motives,* where he gives the three moments traditional designations which are very suggestive: *Poiema, Pathema, Mathema.* They may also be called, for convenience, Purpose, Passion (or Suffering) and Perception. It is this tragic rhythm of action which is the substance or spiritual content of the play, and the clue to its extraordinarily comprehensive form" [*Editor's note*].

historic fact. The figure of Oedipus himself fulfills all the require-
ments of the scapegoat, the dismembered king or god-figure. The situation in which Thebes is presented at the beginning of the play—in
peril of its life; its crops, its herds, its women mysteriously infertile,
signs of a mortal disease of the City, and the disfavor of the gods—is
like the withering which winter brings, and calls, in the same way,
for struggle, dismemberment, death, and renewal. And this tragic sequence is the substance of the play. It is enough to know that myth
and ritual are close together in their genesis, two direct imitations of
the perennial experience of the race.

But when one considers *Oedipus* as a ritual one understands it in
ways which one cannot by thinking of it merely as a dramatization of
a story, even that story. Harrison has shown that the Festival of Dionysos, based ultimately upon the yearly vegetation ceremonies, included *rites de passage,* like that celebrating the assumption of adult-
hood—celebrations of the mystery of individual growth and development. At the same time, it was a prayer for the welfare of the whole
City; and this welfare was understood not only as material prosperity,
but also as the natural order of the family, the ancestors, the present
members, and the generations still to come, and, by the same token,
obedience to the gods who were jealous, each in his own province, of
this natural and divinely sanctioned order and proportion.

We must suppose that Sophocles' audience (the whole population
of the City) came early, prepared to spend the day in the bleachers.
At their feet was the semicircular dancing-ground for the chorus, and
the thrones for the priests, and the altar. Behind that was the raised
platform for the principal actors, backed by the all-purpose, emblem-
atic façade, which would presently be taken to represent Oedipus' palace in Thebes. The actors were not professionals in our sense, but
citizens selected for a religious office, and Sophocles himself had trained
them and the chorus.

This crowd must have had as much appetite for thrills and diver-
sion as the crowds who assemble in our day for football games and
musical comedies, and Sophocles certainly holds the attention with
an exciting show. At the same time his audience must have been alert
for the fine points of poetry and dramaturgy, for *Oedipus* is being offered in competition with other plays on the same bill. But the element which distinguishes this theater, giving it its unique directness
and depth, is the *ritual expectancy* which Sophocles assumed in his
audience. The nearest thing we have to this ritual sense of theater is,
I suppose, to be found at an Easter performance of the *Mattias Passion.* We also can observe something similar in the dances and ritual
mummery of the Pueblo Indians. Sophocles' audience must have been

prepared, like the Indians standing around their plaza, to consider the playing, the make-believe it was about to see—the choral invocations, with dancing and chanting; the reasoned discourses and the terrible combats of the protagonists; the mourning, the rejoicing, and the contemplation of the final stage-picture or epiphany—as imitating and celebrating the mystery of human nature and destiny. And this mystery was at once that of individual growth and development, and that of the precarious life of the human City.

I have indicated how Sophocles presents the life of the mythic Oedipus in the tragic rhythm, the mysterious quest of life. Oedipus is shown seeking his own true being; but at the same time and by the same token, the welfare of the City. When one considers the ritual form of the whole play, it becomes evident that it presents the tragic but perennial, even normal, quest of the whole City for its well-being. In this larger action, Oedipus is only the protagonist, the first and most important champion. This tragic quest is realized by all the characters in their various ways; but in the development of the action as a whole it is the chorus alone that plays a part as important as that of Oedipus; its counterpart, in fact. The chorus holds the balance between Oedipus and his antagonists, marks the progress of their struggles, and restates the main theme, and its new variation, after each dialogue or agon. The ancient ritual was probably performed by a chorus alone without individual developments and variations, and the chorus, in *Oedipus,* is still the element that throws most light on the ritual form of the play as a whole.

The chorus consists of twelve or fifteen "Elders of Thebes." This group is not intended to represent literally all of the citizens either of Thebes or of Athens. The play opens with a large delegation of Theban citizens before Oedipus' palace, and the chorus proper does not enter until after the prologue. Nor does the chorus speak directly for the Athenian audience; we are asked throughout to make-believe that the theater is the agora at Thebes; and at the same time Sophocles' audience is witnessing a ritual. It would, I think, be more accurate to say that the chorus represents the point of view and the faith of Thebes as a whole, and, by analogy, of the Athenian audience. Their errand before Oedipus' palace is like that of Sophocles' audience in the theater: they are watching a sacred combat, in the issue of which they have an all-important and official stake. Thus they represent the audience and the citizens in a particular way—not as a mob formed in response to some momentary feeling, but rather as an organ of a highly self-conscious community: something closer to the "conscience of the race" than to the overheated affectivity of a mob.

According to Aristotle, a Sophoclean chorus is a character that takes an important role in the action of the play, instead of merely making incidental music between the scenes, as in the plays of Euripides. The chorus may be described as a group personality, like an old Parliament. It has its own traditions, habits of thought and feeling, and mode of being. It exists, in a sense, as a living entity, but not with the sharp actuality of an individual. It perceives; but its perception is at once wider and vaguer than that of a single man. It shares, in its way, the seeking action of the play as a whole; but it cannot act in all the modes; it depends upon the chief agonists to invent and try out the detail of policy, just as a rather helpless but critical Parliament depends upon the Prime Minister to act but, in its less specific form of life, survives his destruction.

When the chorus enters after the prologue, with its questions, its invocation of the various gods, and its focus upon the hidden and jeopardized welfare of the City—Athens or Thebes—the list of essential *dramatis personae,* as well as the elements needed to celebrate the ritual, is complete, and the main action can begin. It is the function of the chorus to mark the stages of this action, and to perform the suffering and perceiving part of the tragic rhythm. The protagonist and his antagonists develop the "purpose" with which the tragic sequence begins; the chorus, with its less than individual being, broods over the agons, marks their stages with a word (like that of the chorus leader in the middle of the Tiresias scene), and (expressing its emotions and visions in song and dance) suffers the results, and the new perception at the end of the fight.

The choral odes are lyrics but they are not to be understood as poetry, the art of words, only, for they are intended also to be danced and sung. And though each chorus has its own shape, like that of a discrete lyric—its beginning, middle, and end—it represents also one passion or pathos in the changing action of the whole. This passion, like the other moments in the tragic rhythm, is felt at so general or, rather, so deep a level that it seems to contain both the mob ferocity that Nietzsche felt in it and, at the other extreme, the patience of prayer. It is informed by faith in the unseen order of nature and the gods, and moves through a sequence of modes of suffering. This may be illustrated from the chorus I have quoted at the end of the Tiresias scene.

It begins (close to the savage emotion of the end of the fight) with images suggesting that cruel "Bacchic frenzy" which is supposed to be the common root of tragedy and of the "old" comedy: "In panoply of fire and lightning / The son of Zeus now springs upon him." In the first antistrophe these images come together more clearly as we relish the chase; and the fleeing culprit, as we imagine him, begins to resemble Oedipus, who is lame, and always associated with the rough wilderness of Kithairon. But in the second strophe, as though appalled by its ambivalent feelings and the imagined possibilities, the chorus sinks back into a more dark and patient posture of suffering, "in awe," "hovering in hope." In the second antistrophe this is developed into something like the orthodox Christian attitude of prayer, based on faith, and assuming the possibility of a hitherto unimaginable truth and answer: "Zeus and Apollo are wise," etc. The whole chorus then ends with a new vision of Oedipus, of the culprit, and of the direction in which the welfare of the City is to be sought. This vision is still colored by the chorus's human love of Oedipus as Hero, for the chorus has still its own purgation to complete, cannot as yet accept completely either the suffering in store for it, or Oedipus as scapegoat. But it marks the end of the first complete "purpose-passion-perception" unit, and lays the basis for the new purpose which will begin the next unit.

It is also to be noted that the chorus changes the scene which we, as audience, are to imagine. During the agon between Oedipus and Tiresias, our attention is fixed upon their clash, and the scene is literal, close, and immediate: before Oedipus' palace. When the fighters depart and the choral music starts, the focus suddenly widens, as though we had been removed to a distance. We become aware of the interested City around the bright arena; and beyond that, still more dimly, of Nature, sacred to the hidden gods. Mr. Burke has expounded the fertile notion that human action may be understood in terms of the scene in which it occurs, and vice versa: the scene is defined by the mode of action. The chorus's action is not limited by the sharp, rationalized purposes of the protagonist; its mode of action, more patient, less sharply realized, is cognate with a wider, if less accurate, awareness of the scene of human life. But the chorus's action, as I have remarked, is not that of passion itself (Nietzsche's cosmic void of night) but suffering informed by the faith of the tribe in a human and a divinely sanctioned natural order: "If such deeds as these are honored," the chorus asks after Jocasta's impiety, "why should I dance and sing?" (lines 894, 895). Thus it is one of the most important functions of the chorus to reveal, in its widest and most mysterious extent, the theater of human life which the play, and indeed the whole Festival of Dionysos, assumed. Even when the chorus does not speak, but only watches, it maintains this theme and this perspective—ready to take the whole stage when the fighters depart.

If one thinks of the movement of the play, it appears that the tragic rhythm analyzes human action temporally into successive modes, as a crystal analyzes a white beam of light spatially into the colored bands of the spectrum. The chorus, always present, represents one of these modes, and at the recurrent moments when reasoned purpose is gone, it takes the stage with its faith-informed passion, moving through an ordered succession of modes of suffering, to a new perception of the immediate situation.

Two Questions of Dramatic Form in the
Oedipus Tyrannus

by G. M. Kirkwood

I Sophoclean Drama and Ritual

Everyone knows that the performance of Greek tragedy in the fifth century B.C. was part of a religious ritual in honor of Dionysus and that the plots of Greek tragedy are nearly all drawn from myth. To some literary critics of our time the proximity of myth and ritual to a literary form constitutes an irresistible lure; it has even been maintained that all literary forms can be derived from patterns of myth and ritual. In view of the recent trend among mythologists to find the origin of all myth—or nearly all—in ritual, the temptation to ally ritual myth to the form of Greek tragedy, where we have in the background not only myth but an undeniable context of ritual, becomes powerful. Can this background be usefully exploited in the criticism of Greek tragedy?

That the element of ritual had an effect on the reception of Greek tragedy by its original audience is certain. The atmosphere of a religious celebration, however attenuated or secularized the actual worship has become, is different from that of an evening of theater, and more intense and personal. The very fact that it was a communal affair in which audience as well as playwright and actors participated removes the ancient Greek theater to a special realm.[1] But what about

"Two Questions of Dramatic Form in the Oedipus Tyrannus: *I Sophoclean Drama and Ritual; II Character Portrayal" (editor's title), by G. M. Kirkwood. From* A Study of Sophoclean Drama *(Ithaca: Cornell University Press, 1958), pp. 11–16, 127–35. Copyright © 1958 by Cornell University. Reprinted by permission of Cornell University Press.*

[1] Opstelten, *Pessimism* [J. C. Opstelten, *Sophocles and Greek Pessimism*, trans. J. A. Ross (Amsterdam, 1952)—*Editor's note*], goes at least as far as one can safely go in describing the effect of ritual on the play's reception. In discussing *OT* he has the following: "We should never forget that it was a play staged in honour of Dionysus. . . . While experiencing an inescapable tragic feeling with his eyes and ears, [the spectator] at the same time shared, as the highest climax in the interesting communion of poet, players, and the public, . . . the paradoxical and tremendous

the plays themselves? Can we say that by their very nature they form a significant ritual entity? It may be that in the act of composition and in the act of performance playwright and actors were affected by the religious circumstances of the performance, but this is not the kind of influence that can be used in criticism. What is needed is evidence of the influence of ritual upon the form of the drama, and it is this kind of influence that has been stressed by critics who wish to make ritual a meaningful factor in the criticism of Greek drama. Is there such evidence?

We must carefully distinguish between a ritual origin, which no one would deny to Greek tragedy or to some of its plots, and ritual qualities in the actual plays. Ritual origin is a matter of cultural and literary history, with only a general and critically intangible effect on any one concrete play; ritual elements, if they exist in substantial form, come within the province of the critic in his estimate of an individual play. A recent critic states that "the Cambridge School of Classical Anthropology has shown in great detail that the form of Greek tragedy follows the form of a very ancient ritual" [2]—that of the *eniautos-daimon,* Jane Harrison's seasonal god. We need to distinguish between the theories of the anthropologists and the evidence of the plays; there is no better aid for this distinction than the searching criticism of the anthropologists' theories in A. W. Pickard-Cambridge's *Dithyramb, Tragedy and Comedy,* where the author makes abundantly clear that the gap between theory and evidence is deplorably broad. Gilbert Murray has elaborated, on the basis of anthropological theory, an archetype of tragedy in which the six steps of the ritual of the *eniautos-daimon* exist in proper order; but both the ritual and the daimon are hypothetical, and, above all, Murray's attempt to relate his fictitious archetype to extant plays is a complete and obvious failure. There is no evidence that allows us to suppose that Greek playwrights were consciously or unconsciously adhering to a ritual pattern in the construction, or the spirit, of their plays. They adhered, of course, to the general form of the myths they dramatized; but even supposing that we could assert that all these myths originated in rites, there is no reason to believe that the myths, with one or two possible exceptions, were concerned with the adventures of a year spirit.[3]

---

experience of the Absolute, by the power of which all sensations of littleness and greatness, of death and resurrection, were inextricably combined into one mighty emotion which filled him with a magical transcendence" (p. 63).

[2] Francis Fergusson, *The Idea of a Theater* (Princeton, 1949), 26. All my further quotations from Fergusson are from the chapter in this book on *OT.*

[3] Thirty years or so ago, when the influence of Frazer's *The Golden Bough* was at its zenith, it was usual to ascribe the origin of nearly all religious rituals to the

This kind of ritual influence we must discard as critically unusable. No doubt it is valuable to have a background of knowledge about the origin—the possible origin—of Greek tragedy, but that is all. It will not help in the least to call the Teiresias scene of *Oedipus Tyrannus* an *agon;* we have not the slightest grounds for supposing that it was such in any ritual way.

There is further reason for caution in assessing the importance of ritual in the performance of Greek tragedy. One of the basic elements of ritual is repetition; a ritual formula is sacred and moving precisely because it is unchangeable, because every word, every gesture, has to be just so; performer and audience alike are keenly conscious in advance of every detail that must come. Even assuming what we have no right to suppose, that every Greek tragedy is a repetition of one "Urmyth," the effect of the repetition would not be the effect of ritual, because the story is told so differently each time. We must therefore disagree with Fergusson when he says of Greek tragedy that "the element which distinguishes this theater, giving it its unique directness and depth, is the *ritual expectancy. . . .* The nearest thing we have to this ritual sense of theater . . . [is] an Easter performance of the *Mattias Passion.*" [4] It need hardly be pointed out that the ritual ele-

---

worship of year spirits. Since then the situation among anthropologists and comparative religionists has changed; the influence of Arnold van Gennep's *Les rites de passage* (Paris, 1909) and of later similar theories has outstripped the Frazerian view, and it is now fashionable to ascribe the origin of nearly all religious rituals to initiation ceremonies. Even the worship of such a favorite *eniautos-daimon* as Dionysus has recently been declared to contain substantial elements of initiation ceremonies. (Cf. H. Jeanmaire, *Dionysus* [Paris, 1951]). In a general survey of the present state of research in Greek mythology Fernand Chapouthier ("De l'avenir des études sur la mythologie grecque," *Actes du Premier Congrès de la Fédération Internationale des Associations d'Etudes Classiques* [Paris, 1951], 259–67) observes that the interpretation of myth has in the course of the past century made its way from heaven (the solar mythology of Max Müller) to earth (the year spirits and earth mothers), and now to what lies between—man (initiation rites). The notion that ritual underlies myth has also been questioned, and excellent evidence has been produced to show that either myth or ritual may give rise to the other, or either may develop and flourish without the other. (Cf. Clyde Kluckhohn, "Myths and Rituals: A General Theory," *HTR*, 35 [1942], 45–79.)

It follows that in making assumptions about the nature of myth and ritual literary critics would do well to proceed with extreme caution and to be wary about accepting any theory as the final and incontrovertible word. In the case of Greek tragedy the ritual origin and nature of the occasion of performance, the Dionysia, are not open to doubt. (For the ancient evidence, see Pickard-Cambridge, *Dithyramb, Tragedy and Comedy, passim.*) But the connection between these matters and the origin and nature of the form of individual dramas and their myths is wholly uncertain. For Murray's theory, see Jane Harrison, *Themis* (Cambridge, 1912), Ch. viii, Appendix.

[4] See above, p. 58 [*Editor's note*].

ment, that which permits "ritual expectancy" in an Easter performance of the *Mattias Passion,* lies in the fact that it is a performance
of the same religious work at the same festival time and again; if
Greek tragedy consisted of an annual performance, at the Dionysia,
of Euripides' *Bacchae,* this analogy of Fergusson's would hold good.[5]
But Greek tragic performances consisted of the presentation of a large
number of very different plays at the Dionysia. All we can salvage of
ritual in Greek tragedy is (*a*) that the occasion of performance was a
ritual, which made its mark on the atmosphere of the performance, and
(*b*) that, probably, some of the myths dramatized were ultimately of
ritual origin; but of the nature and meaning of the original rites we
know virtually nothing—not even what aspects of life the rites were
concerned with.

I have labored this point for two reasons: first, because the study of
myth and ritual in relation to literary form and meaning has lately
become a subject of deep and growing interest to many critics, and
therefore it is well, in discussing a Greek dramatist, to assess at the
outset the value of such an approach to Greek tragedy; secondly, the
question of myth (and thus implicitly though very indirectly of ritual)
has a special significance for Sophocles among the Greek dramatists.
Since I have hitherto quoted Fergusson's book only to disagree with
it, let me conclude this matter with a sentence of his that has my approval. He speaks of "the prerational image of human nature and
destiny which the ritual conveyed; which Sophocles felt as still alive
and significant for his generation." Here is a matter that is real in
Sophocles, and significant for the criticism of his plays. I am not sure
about the notion of prerationality and would substitute "myth" for
"ritual"; with these provisos, I believe that this sentence describes an
important element in Sophocles' dramatic method and helps to distinguish him from his two great compeers: Sophocles, in his plays, "thinks
mythically," that is, he keeps himself within the confines of the tradi-

[5] The same objection obtains, far more strongly, in the case of Fergusson's further
"analogy": "We can also observe something similar in the dances and ritual mummery of the Pueblo Indians" (p. 28). According to Ruth Benedict (*Patterns of Culture,* 55), the Pueblo Indians are zealously devoted to the exact reproductions of
traditional rites. Therefore in spirit they are almost directly opposite to the Athenians of the fifth century B.C. In our excitement at finding that the ancient Greeks
had rites and traditions in their religious and social life for which parallels can be
found in other cultures, we must not forget that one great and historically important distinguishing mark of ancient Greek artists was their capacity to transcend
tradition without at once abandoning it.
A closer analogy would be the performance of various works, written by different
composers, at Easter. This analogy would of course minimize the effect of ritual on
any single work, and even it would not be quite on the mark, because the celebration of the Dionysia had no such religious pre-eminence as the celebration of
Easter.

tional mythological setting in a way that is foreign to Aeschylus with his creative use of myth and to Euripides with his critical use of myth.

II Character Portrayal

In this play there is no basic pair of characters as in the diptych plays, but the importance of character interaction for the revelation of the theme is no slighter. Another kind of contrast contributes greatly to the action of the play, a contrast between the revealed and the unrevealed or, as Reinhardt puts it, between seeming and reality.[1] In the customary Sophoclean manner this contrast is joined with one of will and personality: while Oedipus strives constantly to cut through the mystery and know the truth, a whole series of persons tries to hide the truth from him—Teiresias, Jocasta, the Theban herdsman, and, in the time before the action, Oedipus' Corinthian foster parents. The theme is centered in the person of Oedipus, and the function of the subordinate persons is to reveal his nature. We must consider in detail three of these persons, Creon, Jocasta, and Teiresias. The relationship of each of them to Oedipus is a work of dramatic genius.

The first major interplay of character is in Oedipus' scene with Teiresias; but in the prologue there is some contrast between the magnificent and self-confident king and the respectful but eminently god-fearing priest who speaks for the Theban people. The priest very explicitly differentiates his respect for Oedipus from his piety to the gods (31); and in referring to Oedipus' victory over the Sphinx he does not fail to mention the aid of heaven (38). Oedipus, by the end of the prologue, has become most vehement in his promises of what *he* will do: he will be the avenger of the land and of Apollo too (136); he for his own sake will rid Thebes of the pestilence (138, note the touch of egotism suggested by the expression αὐτὸς αὐτοῦ); he, in fact, will do all (145).[2] His final words soften the effect of complete self-reliance somewhat (σὺν τῷ θεῷ, 146), but there is an air of dominant confidence that differs markedly from the piety of the priest, whose last words recall once more this spirit when he calls upon Apollo, sender of the oracle, to be the deliverer (147–50). We must not cry *hybris;* up to this point, at least, Oedipus is not guilty of any impropriety of spirit. But neither must we disregard the clear meaning of this initial slight

[1] *Sophokles* [Karl Reinhardt, *Sophokles*, 3rd ed. (Frankfurt am Main, 1947)—*Editor's note*], 108 and *passim* in his chapter on *OT* [translated in part above, pp. 49–56].

[2] ὡς πᾶν ἐμοῦ δράσοντος. The usual sinister meaning of πάντα δρᾶν is not to be forgotten here. This is among the first of the many striking verbal ironies of the play.

constrast of spirit; it is a significant hint of the powerful and impetuous self-reliance that marks Oedipus' nature as it is revealed later in
the play.

We have seen the structural principle of Oedipus' scene with Teiresias in operation twice before, in the Creon-Haemon and the Creon-
Teiresias scenes of *Antigone,* but the present scene is much bolder in
execution than either of the others and, because of the infinitely greater
stature of Oedipus than Creon, far more engrossing. Here, following the
pattern of the earlier scenes, the prophet begins well intentioned, the
king respectful and calm. Indeed the extreme reverence of Oedipus
toward Teiresias (he addresses him as σωτήρ and ἄναξ and declares ἐν
σοὶ ἐσμεν) is very unlike his imperious manner in the prologue and his
anger later in the scene. It is quite clear that Sophocles is aiming at
a striking contrast between the mood at the beginning of the scene
and that at its end. (In this too the pattern follows the *Antigone* scenes
—in this case the Creon-Haemon scene especially—but again the *OT*
scene has a great deal more verve.) Oedipus, obstructed by Teiresias'
refusal to talk, soon flies into a terrible rage (334–35) and presently
accuses him of complicity in the crime (348–49). This in turn stings
Teiresias into declaring that Oedipus is himself the murderer that he
seeks. By now Oedipus is in a towering rage, and Teiresias can shout
aloud the whole truth without any chance of Oedipus' discovering it:
the two men are moving in different channels of thought, though each
is impelled in the direction he takes by the influence of the other.
Oedipus hears Teiresias and reacts, and yet he does not really hear.
Or does he? Is there, behind the indignation and rage that fill this
scene and the next, with Creon, a lurking fear that what Teiresias has
said is right? If so, it is a less explicit fear than that which Sophocles
makes us realize that Creon feels in *Antigone,* where we know from his
behavior at the end of his scenes with Haemon and Teiresias that his
angry self-defense has no firm inner conviction. With Oedipus, the
fear, if such there is, is deep within and unconscious.

The revelation of Oedipus' anger and his too ready suspicion of
Teiresias have implications for the character of Oedipus that are not
to be disregarded. Toward the end of the scene there is a subtle and
most revealing display of Oedipus' egotism. A reference by Teiresias
(436) to the parents of Oedipus catches the king's conscious ear, though
the foregoing declarations of his guilt have found him apparently deaf.
Oedipus is for the moment all attention (437), and we think that now
he must learn his parentage. But the prophet answers enigmatically
(438), and Oedipus reproaches him for doing so (439). Teiresias asks
if solving enigmas is not Oedipus' special skill (440); and this reminder
of his triumph over the Sphinx so engrosses the king's attention that

he forgets all about his original question and the moment of possible revelation passes unfulfilled.

The contrast between the outward magnificence and inward blindness of Oedipus and the outward blindness and inward sight of the prophet is one of the given attributes of the scene, and Sophocles does not waste this natural opportunity. (Comparison with *Antigone* is instructive: there, though the same opportunity existed, Sophocles did not use it. This is one measure of the difference between the Creon of *Antigone* and the Oedipus of *OT*. Creon is not great enough for the irony to be dramatically telling; Oedipus is.) Oedipus taunts Teiresias with his blindness, saying that he has "eyes for profit only, blindness in his craft" (388–89); Teiresias' answer is a magnificent consummation of this play on sight and blindness:

σὺ καὶ δέδορκας κοὐ βλέπεις ἵν' εἶ κακοῦ.   [413]

[You have your sight, but you do not see in what evil you are.]

With Creon, Oedipus has two scenes, and the second is no less important than the first for its revelation of Oedipus, though its effect is easier to overlook. The first follows the Teiresias-scene and is like it in form, though Creon has not the fire and authority of the old prophet and hence the dramatic pitch of the scene is much lower. Creon, as everybody knows, is the moderate man. His role is to stress, by his unfailing modesty and calm, the extravagance of speech and the self-reliance displayed by Oedipus. This aspect of their relationship needs little mention. Oedipus is angry from the start; Creon pleads only for a fair hearing (543–44). In contrast to Oedipus with his wild suspicions and guesses, Creon is a model of caution; typical of him is the statement, in answer to a question, "I do not know; and what I do not know, it is not my habit to assert" (569). In his long speech (583–615) the burden of Creon's argument is that any man of modesty would prefer to enjoy a ruler's power without the cares of rule, as he does. All he wants is τὰ σὺν κέρδει καλά [honors that bring gain] (595). Oedipus is arrogant in his unjust charges: Creon is "clearly" the murderer of Laius (534); he has been "caught" plotting against the person of Oedipus (642–43). That Creon, mild of manner, loyal, patient, should be painted such a monster is striking proof of the stubborn reliance of Oedipus on his own convictions. The Creon he is battling is a figment of his imagination.[3]

In their second scene, at the end of the play, there is the same con-

---

[3] The behavior of Oedipus in this scene is surely proof enough that the Oedipus of this play is not faultless. The fact that Oedipus' suspicions of Creon begin in the prologue (124–25) does not appreciably modify the effect of this later attack.

trast, though its emphasis is different. Creon is still the man of complete moderation, Oedipus the extremist; but now it is himself that Oedipus attacks, while toward Creon his attitude is one of humility and gratitude. The change emphasizes, of course, the completeness of Oedipus' reversal of fortune, and it shows that he is as capable of generosity as of abuse—which we already know, I think, without this demonstration.

Creon thus serves as a pivot about which Oedipus turns in his contrasting phases of self-confidence and abasement. But his usefulness as a foil for Oedipus has more depth than this. For all his unfailing justness and moderation Creon is not a character who excites our sympathy. His virtues are a little mechanical; there is no sign of an inward fire of conviction. This aspect of his nature is especially clear at the end of the play, but even in his earlier self-defense his impersonal logicality fails to stir us, especially in contrast with Oedipus' emotional intensity. To give one small example of this difference: when Oedipus, convinced of Creon's treachery, shouts, "My city, alas for my city" (629)! Creon very correctly, coolly, and logically answers, "I too have a share in the city; it is not yours alone." Oedipus is all wrong; his words are neither just nor logical; Creon's are both. Yet by its fervor the unjust cry of Oedipus excites more sympathy than the dispassionate truth of Creon.

In the final scene of the play this thread of contrast is more apparent, and the playwright's purpose in so arranging matters is quite clear: it is a means of ensuring continued domination (dramatic, that is) by the tragic hero. It is striking that Creon at no time gives a sign of emotion for the fall of Oedipus. If he were a meaner man than he is, he would be elated; if a greater, there would be some show of sympathy. But when Oedipus begs to be cast forth at once from Thebes (1436–37), Creon answers, "I should have done so already, had I not thought it best to consult the gods first." Creon will do nothing without assurance that it is the right thing; but he is quite prepared to drive out his blind and helpless kinsman without the least personal feeling. Just at the end Oedipus pleads, hopelessly of course, that his daughters may stay with him (1522). Creon answers: πάντα μὴ βούλου κρατεῖν [do not wish to rule in all things]. The reproach is slight, and no doubt justified; but its total want of feeling is vaguely offensive. Creon is not malignant,[4] he is well intentioned. Of his own accord he brings Oedipus' daughters to him. But he is colorless, without depths of good or evil. His sameness is symbolized by his repetition, at the end, of the characteristic sentence (569) quoted above; at the end, in answer to the impetuous questioning of Oedipus, he answers:

[4] The scoundrelly Creon of *OC* should not influence our view of the Creon of *OT*. The two characters are quite separate.

ἃ μὴ φρονῶ γὰρ οὐ φιλῶ λέγειν μάτην.   [1520]

[When I lack knowledge, it is not my habit to speak to no purpose.]

Were Creon a more living and attractive figure, the sympathy and admiration of the audience would be less wholly Oedipus'. In one important way the relationship is like that of Ajax and Odysseus, though Odysseus is a much more attractive figure than Creon: in both cases the distinction between the high spirit of the central figure and his unheroic foil is firmly drawn.

The relation between Oedipus and Jocasta is mainly one of sympathy. The skepticism of Oedipus, which appears in his scene with Teiresias when in his rage he casts slurs on the ability and honesty of Teiresias, is shared by Jocasta. Indeed she serves as a temptress, at the end of Episode Two and in Episode Three, to induce Oedipus to disregard the ominous oracles and trust in his own judgment entirely. But we need not interpret Jocasta as a prototype of the free-thinking "liberated" intellectual Athenian woman of Sophocles' day;[5] her skepticism springs from her own immediate situation, from her desire to protect Oedipus and keep peace; not self-confidence, but love, governs her attitude. Three times she speaks out against the validity of oracles (707–25, 857–58, 952–53), twice drawing Oedipus after her. Of the folly of their skepticism and the ultimate vindication of the oracles it is hardly necessary to speak. But does Sophocles present their skepticism as a thing to be condemned or is his use of oracles here purely a dramaturgical convenience? We have already noticed, in Chapter II, the skill with which Sophocles uses oracles in his plays, and it was suggested there that we cannot be certain about Sophocles' own attitude toward the religious significance of oracles. This much perhaps we can say of the present instance: the skepticism of Oedipus is a symbol, not necessarily of impiety, but of confidence in the self-sufficiency of human power; and in Sophocles' view human power is inadequate armor to protect against suffering.

In any case, the skepticism of Oedipus and Jocasta creates telling dramatic suspense. Several times Jocasta is used as a parallel and prelude to the fortunes of Oedipus. First she sees that the oracles are true after all, and later he too sees it. First she finds her life ruined by the inevitable process of events, and later he comes to the same terrible knowledge. We noticed above how the dramatist uses the difference in their reception of the Corinthian messenger's revelation of Oedipus' origin: the knowledge and despair of Jocasta are contrasted with the blind excitement of Oedipus. The most striking case of a contrast and parallel between Jocasta and Oedipus is in their successive encounters

[5] This is done by [Max] Pohlenz, [*Die*] *Griechische Tragödie,*[2] [(Göttingen, 1954) —*Editor's additions*], 219.

with Τύχη. When the Corinthian has brought news of Polybus' death, news that seems to confound the oracle that Oedipus will slay his father, Jocasta, in the excitement of her relief, cries: "Why should a man have fears? His life is under Tyche's sway; there is no certain knowledge in advance. It is best to live at random, in whatever way one can" (977–79). By the end of the episode Jocasta has realized that not Tyche but an inexorable chain of events is in command of her life and that of Oedipus; and she goes into the palace to hang herself in despair. But now Oedipus takes up the theme; baffled as to who his parents are (now that the Corinthian has told him that he is not the son of Polybus and Merope) and wildly excited by the search for truth, in the last speech of the episode Oedipus cries that he is "Fortune's child" (παῖδα τῆς Τύχης, 1080).[6] In the next short episode he arrives at the dreadful knowledge in which Jocasta has anticipated him.

A few words on the relationship between two minor figures, the Corinthian and the herdsman, will bring us to the end of our review of character relationships in this play. They are clearly differentiated. The Corinthian, who comes as the bearer of what he is confident are good tidings, has been shown in the episode before they meet to be a cheery, familiar, rather garrulous soul; the herdsman, knowing that he possesses a dreadful secret about his monarch, is trying desperately to hide it and is therefore surly and slow to speak, just the reverse of the Corinthian. The opposite pull of these two characters brings a remarkable tension to this crucial scene. The blithe Corinthian, unaware of the horrors that he is bringing to light, is helpfully jogging the memory of the reluctant herdsman. With naïve self-satisfaction he says the terrible, irrevocable words: "Here he is, ὦ τᾶν, here before you is the babe of yore" (1145)! The Corinthian's colloquial address, his cheery delivery of the fatal message, and his obliviousness of the herdsman's desperate efforts to conceal his knowledge add enormously to the grimness of the moment. Here is a *very* brief instance of the tragic use of comedy, in the Greek style.

It would be false to suggest that these character relationships are the whole of *Oedipus Tyrannus,* or that to ponder the relationships as *disiecta membra* is the proper way to receive the play. On the contrary, the effect of the play is both unified and poetic. What I wish to suggest here is that the towering figure of Oedipus and the seemingly inevitable tension of the action are raised on a substructure of count-

---

[6] Whitman, *Sophocles* [Cedric H. Whitman, *Sophocles, a Study of Heroic Humanism* (Cambridge, Mass., 1951)—*Editor's note*], 145, cites this speech of Oedipus as evidence of a new spirit, much enlarged upon by Sophocles in subsequent plays, the spirit of heroic endurance. The suggestion is interesting and probably correct, but the passage has also a dramatic point entirely within the play, as a parallel to Jocasta's words on Tyche.

less small but carefully designed details of characterization. There is no other play of Sophocles where the power of the drama seems to spring so naturally from the person of the tragic hero and the nature of the situation, as if scarcely any intervention by the dramatist were necessary; and there is no play of Sophocles in which the playwright's consummate genius in the manipulation of characters is more fully in operation.

Sophoclean Rulers: Oedipus

by Victor Ehrenberg

It has frequently been observed that there is much likeness between Creon in *Antigone* and Oedipus in *Oedipus Tyrannus,* even though "Oedipus is the good ruler in spite of his defects, and Creon the bad ruler in spite of his virtues." [1] Oedipus is a "good king," a father of his people, an honest and great ruler, while at the same time an outstanding intellect. The Polis is always in his mind,[2] he regards his position as a gift entrusted to him by the free decision of the citizens (383), and his final care is not for himself but for the people and the State (314f, 443). When his authority is questioned by Creon's quiet resistance, he feels it like treason of the Polis to himself; that must be the meaning of the outcry: "Oh Polis, Polis!" (629). He even shares the throne, not only with his wife who had been his predecessor's wife (579), and in her quality as queen and co-regent merely adds to his own dignity and greatness; Creon, too, is his co-regent, a fact that shows that Oedipus shuns autocratic appearances. He is also a pious man who believes in oracles, respects the bonds of family, fears and hates impurity. The whole plot, and the very tragedy of the man Oedipus, are based on the fact of his piety.[3]

The same man, however, is called "tyrant." The Greek word is, of course, ambiguous, and it is justifiable to translate the title of the play, in which *Tyrannus,* at any rate, is a later addition, as *Oedipus the King.* In the play, *tyrannis* sometimes simply means kingship (128, 380, 1095). On the other hand, Oedipus has a very clear feeling for the outstanding importance and high dignity of his royal position and of kings in general (128f, 257ff, 267f). He is a great man, and he him-

[1] Webster [T. B. L. Webster, *An Introduction to Sophocles* (Oxford, 1936)—*Editor's note*], 63. Cf. also C. Robert, *Oidipus,* pp. 347 f.

[2] Cf. 302, 312, 322, 331, 340, 629.

[3] Cf. J. T. Sheppard's edition, p. xxvii.

self knows it (8), a man who likes to give orders and to hear himself doing so (226, 235, 252). He describes his position in almost the same words as Creon (237 = *Ant.* 173),[4] words which show that in his heart he wants full and absolute authority. The same tendency becomes manifest in the attitude of those who are ruled by him. The suppliant people approach him almost as a god (2, 31f), and he is honoured as a saviour, as *Soter* (46ff). Such honours, as every Greek knew, are dangerous, for they may lead to *hybris*. A great man in the position of a king was more likely than anyone else to overstep the bounds set to human beings by the gods.

Oedipus is indeed threatened with danger and temptation. The king is on the verge of tyranny. The scene with Creon (513ff) reveals this with full clarity, and the likeness between Oedipus and the Creon of the *Antigone* becomes very close. There is the same blind suspicion even towards friends, the same inclination to hasty inferences, the same rash vindictiveness. When Oedipus meets opposition, or thinks he does, he easily loses all self-control; his treatment of the old herdsman in a later scene is outrageous (1152ff). He is in danger of acquiring the moral qualities of a tyrant, and his position and greatness are bound to lead to political tyranny. Again very much like Creon, he identifies himself with the State and upholds the principle of monarchic rule even if the ruler is bad (629). Creon, who in the *OT.* represents moderation and common sense, has to remind him that the Polis does not belong to him alone (630). Even the blinded and desperate Oedipus meets the reproach (1522): "Do not crave to be master in everything."

The parallelism between the two plays is most obvious in the two Teiresias scenes, although in the later play it all seems to be transferred to a more fundamental level. Like Creon, Oedipus mistrusts the venerable seer, and suspects him of being bribed (379ff). This is of even greater significance here as the questioning of the truth of oracles and prophetic words is at the core of the plot and, at the same time, contrasts with Oedipus' genuine piety. Oedipus first addresses Teiresias reverently with titles such as *prostates, soter, anax* (304f) which seem more proper to himself; but his attitude changes suddenly and completely when he senses danger to his kingship and to the State

---

[4] Mr. (now Sir John) Sheppard, who gives an excellent exposition of "Oedipus the Tyrant," finds Oedipus' γῆς τῆσδ', ἧς ἐγὼ κράτη τε καὶ θρόνους νέμω [of this land, whose sovereignty and whose throne I control] less overbearing than Creon's ἐγὼ κράτη δὴ πάντα καὶ θρόνους ἔχω [all sovereignty and the throne I now possess], particularly because νέμω [I control] here has not the effect of ἔχω [I possess] there. Still, Zeus is addressed (201): ἀστραπᾶν κράτη νέμων [controlling the powers of the lightning]. Sheppard's distinction, though too subtle, is supported by the general difference between Creon and Oedipus; but the similarity of the two passages is more obvious and more important than the difference.

(330f). His piety fails as soon as his political position, his uncontested leadership of the State, is concerned. This is no petty fear for his own security and power nor, on the other hand, the anger of insulted pride. Oedipus' savage hostility is roused, first by Teiresias' silence which in that moment of dire emergency seems insult and injury alike to the State; it is increased afterwards by the charge that he, the great king and saviour of the State, is in fact the sinner who pollutes and destroys it. Polis and kingship are threatened, and in them Oedipus' deepest concerns. Oedipus the ruler, in spite of his piety, belongs to the world of politics and human standards rather than to the divine order of the world.

Oedipus opposes the seer's prophecy with arguments of his own reasoning (394ff. Self-confident pride in his own wisdom is an outstanding feature of his character from the beginning—we may suppose, ever since he succeeded in solving the riddle of the Sphinx. He probably would agree with the priest that he had achieved this "with the aid of a god" (38), for he equally puts his and the citizens' fate under the ultimate decision of "the god" (146). The man who sets out on his new task by sending first for the venerable seer (287ff) is not lacking in pious reverence; but all we see of him in the play shows unrestrained pride in his own intellectual achievements. No seer found the solution, this is Oedipus' boast; no bird, no god revealed it to him; he, "the utterly ignorant," had to come, and to hit the mark by his own wit (395ff).[5] Pride and self-confidence induce Oedipus to despise prophecy, and to feel almost superior to the gods. He tells the people who pray for deliverance from the plague that they may hope to find their prayers fulfilled, if they listen to him and follow his advice (216f). The struggle between true wisdom and self-confident intellectual pride (cf. 316, 396), well known from *Antigone,* is repeated. Oedipus' scornful refusal of both Creon's advice and Teiresias' prophecy corresponds to Creon's attitude towards Haemon and Teiresias. Lack of true wisdom is an essential feature in the man who is always on the verge of becoming an impious tyrant.

Nevertheless, all this does not make Oedipus morally guilty. He is not an example of *hybris,* but a truly great man, far superior to the king Creon in character as well as in intellect. He suffers because he has done, however unwittingly, what is against the laws of the gods. He who has slain his father and married his mother can never be called "innocent." It has rightly been said that conceptions such as guilt and innocence simply have no meaning here. What matters is

---

[5] I cannot accept Sheppard's theory that Oedipus only gradually, while the play is in progress, becomes so dangerously self-confident and tyrannical. There is no psychological development, but a character in which all the time piety and moderation are on the verge of impiety and tyranny.

that horrible deeds have been committed according to divine prediction, and thus human greatness is set against divine power. This human greatness comes about as the result of the proud self-reliance of a man in power.

Oedipus' self-confident and independent mind displays its full strength in the speech in which he calls himself the son of Tyche (1076ff). In his quest for truth he has come to the final stage when the secret of his birth is to be disclosed. He is great enough to face everything, though he can think of nothing worse than a base origin. He is even more convinced of his own worth than of that of royal kinship; in facing the worst, he turns it into another sign of his own greatness. Tyche is his true mother, and the kings are forgotten. Once he had brought Tyche, "Chance," to Thebes "with good omen" (52), that same "Saviour Chance" which he expects to come through Creon's message from Delphi (80). But it is also Tyche that in Iocaste's words has undone the divine prophecies (949, 977), and, in Oedipus' own words, Tyche killed Laius before he begot a son who might kill him (263). To the audience who knew better these utterances were full of tragic irony, and Tyche must have appeared as a fatal and disastrous power. In fact, she did not only appear as such a power, she was it. In speaking of her, Oedipus unsuspectingly touches on the truth, the gods' cruel game with his life. He calls her the giver of good (1081), not because he forgets that she gives evil as well, but because he believes that Chance has been friendly to him up to now. The months are his brothers, "born with me" (1082); they have accompanied his rise. Like them he is a child of Time and Nature: τῆς γὰρ πέφυκα μητρός [for she is my mother].

It seems clear that Tyche is not yet the changeable, if frightening, though also protecting, deity of a later age which was both sceptical and despondent.[6] It is equally clear that Oedipus, in claiming to be a son of Chance, has gone beyond the bounds of tradition and religion. At that moment, he is only just entering the circle of increasing knowledge about himself. He realizes that his life is ruled by outer forces, but he does not yet realize their tremendous and cruel power. The foundations of his life have gone, but his great and powerful mind knows of no despair. He still relies on his own genius, and it is indeed the very core of his tragedy that, by using his high intellect honestly and uncompromisingly, he brings doom upon himself.

Oedipus does not stand alone. Iocaste's love and anxiety are always

---

[6] Nilsson, *Gesch. d. griech. Religion*, I 713, discovers in *OT.* "den späteren Tyche-begriff," and finds it equally in *Ant.* 1158 and *Ai.* 485, though not in the θεία τύχη of *Phil.* 1316f, 1326 and frg. 196. I do not think he does justice to the tragic element in Sophocles. For a full discussion of the "Son of Tyche" see Diono, *Dioniso*, XV (1952), 56 ff.

at his side. It is her tragedy that she actively leads Oedipus towards their common disaster, and that she realizes the truth gradually though always in advance of him. Modern scholars sometimes describe her as frivolous. That will not do, but the reactions against such a view have, we believe, gone too far and neglected true evidence. When Iocaste tells the story of the oracle given to Laius she speaks of "an oracle—I do not say, from Phoebus himself, but from his ministers" (711). Pointing to the course of events which apparently has proved this oracle to be false, she again distinguishes between the god and the mantic words. It was not necessarily a sign of impiety to admit that seers sometimes made mistakes; the chorus had expressed the same thought before (500),[7] and such scepticism could even turn against the sacred priests of Delphi. Iocaste, however, by distinguishing between the god and the priest, shows that she is aware of the impiety implied in her words. We also ask: why does she mistrust? Jebb thought that it was due to the shock when her firstborn child was sacrificed without saving Laius' life; but there is not the slightest indication that this was so, and her story of both Laius' and the child's fates shows no emotion. We are to understand that her new husband and the children she had from him have made the earlier events of her life things of a remote and detached past. Iocaste, in fact, is satisfied that the oracle was false, because she believes she knows better. Hers is a matter-of-fact way of reasoning, which is not sufficiently explained by her love for Oedipus.

When she mentions the story again (851), it is the god himself whom she blames. No restraint is left. Although her advice to disregard all prophecies (857f) springs from her love for Oedipus, a love which is indeed as much a mother's as a wife's love, this is no explanation for her more manifest impiety. The oracle is still the same, and it might have been easier to convince Oedipus of its untruth if she had again made the priests responsible, and not the god. The fact that she cares more for Oedipus than for anything else may, to some extent, explain and "excuse" her scepticism and blasphemy, but it does not remove them. Her scepticism may spring from her heart rather than her brain; but the very fact that she is so full of love for her husband that she neglects and even despises the gods, is ample proof that, in her emotions as well as her intellect, she has no religion. Her life is an unparalleled tragedy indeed; but she is at the same time truly impious. Her public prayer to Apollo is dictated by the fear which Oedipus' fears have raised in her (917); it is little more than an act of conventional duty, as her own words confirm (911f). When the news of Polybus' death arrives she does not thank the gods,

[7] Cf. p. 27 [in Ehrenberg, *Sophocles and Pericles—Editor's note*].

but again, and with even more scorn than before, she denounces "the prophecies of the gods" (947). She tries to quell Oedipus' fears by explaining away the oracle with a rationalistic allusion to certain dreams (980ff). By this anticipation of psycho-analysis, one of the most amazing and most significant proofs of the poet's insight as well as his purpose, she denies any belief in divine signs. It is only consistent with this that her impiety culminates in her claim that human beings have nothing to fear because their life is determined by the changes of Tyche; no foresight exists, and to live at random is best (977ff). Haunted by fears as she is, fervently wishing to dispel Oedipus' growing suspicions and to divert his searching mind, she ultimately proclaims the law of lawlessness and complete disregard of the gods and their warnings.

Iocaste is "ruling the land with an equal share" (γῆς ἴσον νέμων, 579). This does not mean that she actually takes part in government; her share in the throne is different from Creon's. What it implies is that the thoughts and actions of Oedipus and Iocaste cannot really be separated; for the description of rulership they are one and the same. Her belief ends where his ends too, in replacing the gods by Tyche, in putting sceptical fatalism in the place of piety. Iocaste always proceeds to the extreme possibilities—in hope and joy as well as in disaster—when he is still reluctant and restrained; but he always tries to comply with her thoughts. We shall not be far off the truth if we feel in some of Oedipus' words that he spoke to the woman who was his mother. This crucial fact, which can never be mentioned during the play and is nevertheless always remembered, overshadows their mutual relationship without their knowing. Whatever explanation may be accepted for Iocaste's attitude to the gods, it will not explain what is behind and beyond it. She cannot be truly pious, and her scepticism is, as it were, necessary because she is bound to perish on account of her incest. She shares Oedipus' life and tragedy as the one person who loves him most and who is most loved by him. She, too, is in a moral sense neither guilty nor innocent. What she shows and stands for, more determinedly and more outrageously than he, is that they both belong to a world of man-made standards—the world indeed to which the poet is opposed with heart and soul. Piety is not sufficient, if it is not the unconditional acceptance of one's fate at the hands of the gods.

Iocaste's fate underlines that of Oedipus. So does the great song of the chorus on "the laws set up on high" (863ff), a true parallel to the song on man's greatness in *Antigone*. We have mentioned the song before, but not yet spoken of its bearing on Oedipus. It has been convincingly shown[8] that the song, and in particular the denuncia-

---

[8] Again in Sheppard's edition.

tion of the tyrant, are relevant to Oedipus and Iocaste. The song begins with a prayer for purity and reverence, clearly an answer to Oedipus' and Iocaste's doubts about the oracles; it ends with an even more striking expression of fear of what will happen if the truth of the divine oracles is denied.[9] Between the first and the last stanzas the chorus describes the man who is born of *hybris,* such *hybris* as is displayed by king and queen. This description follows to a large extent the conventional picture of the tyrant, mentioning his pride, greed and irreverence. Not every feature fits the character of Oedipus; but to expect that would not only be pedantic, it would be mistaken. The chorus fears that he who behaves with presumptuous pride and self-confidence will turn tyrannical and impious, and they foresee that Zeus, the true king of the world, will punish the sins of the mortal king. If he does not do so, all religion will become meaningless, and all will be lost. Not only the chorus is afraid of this; we can say that it is the poet himself who expresses his highly emotional and pious beliefs and, although in terms of a conventional nature, depicts the grave dangers threatening his world. To Sophocles the tragedy of Oedipus, as foreseen in this song of despair, is essentially another example of the struggle between divine and human order. In this play neither the divine nor the human world have an outstanding protagonist of their own. The struggle is fought within Oedipus' soul and life as they waver between the duties of a good king and the sins of a tyrant, and between piety and impiety. It is Chance as the expression of the inscrutable will of the gods that eventually destroys Oedipus. That means that his ultimate unbelief is turned into truth against him, a climax of tragic irony.

[9] I am convinced that this song refutes the attempt to take Iocaste's sacrifice to Apollo as a genuine proof that "she is no sceptic or unbeliever" (Bowra [C. M. Bowra, *Sophoclean Tragedy* (Oxford, 1944)—*Editor's note*], 204).

The *Oedipus Tyrannus* and
Greek Archaic Thought

by R. P. Winnington-Ingram

The *Oedipus Tyrannus* holds a special place in the work of Sophocles. The most powerful of his tragedies, it distils the essence of one aspect of his thought, itself a legacy from the archaic age. I refer to the breach between the divine and human modes of existence, the frailty of man and his dependence upon a god-given destiny. This thought receives its classical statement in the first stanza of the ode which the Chorus sing, when Oedipus leaves the stage having learnt the truth about his life. "What man wins more of happiness (*eudaimonia*) than just a semblance and, after the semblance, a decline? I call no mortal blessed, for I have the example of your *daimon*, Oedipus, before my eyes." [1] What do they mean—what did Sophocles mean —by the *daimon* of Oedipus? And by *eudaimonia?* Certainly more by *eudaimonia* than Aristotle meant, when he said that this was the good at which all men aim; and more by *daimon* than we mean, when we speak vaguely of a man's destiny. To quote Dodds again:[2] "A third type of daemon, who makes his first appearance in the Archaic Age, is attached to a particular individual, usually from birth, and determines, wholly or in part, his individual destiny. . . . He represents the individual *moira* or 'portion' of which Homer speaks, but in the personal form which appealed to the imagination

[1] τὸν σὸν τοι παράδειγμ' ἔχων,
    τὸν σὸν δαίμονα, τὸν σόν, ὦ
    τλᾶμον Οἰδιπόδα, βροτῶν
    οὐδὲν μακαρίζω. (1193–6)

[2] Op. cit. [E. R. Dodds, *The Greeks and the Irrational* (Berkeley and Los Angeles, 1951)—*Editor's note*], 42. On *daimon* in Sophocles cf. G. M. Kirkwood, *A Study of Sophoclean Drama,* 185 f.

of the time." The fate of Oedipus, then, is ascribed to a malign
superhuman power which had attended him from birth. Surely this
provides no evidence of independent thought in Sophocles—or of
anything but popular fatalism with superstitious overtones?

The idea of malignity does not indeed occur in the stanza. But
let us go back a little in the play. To set the fears of Oedipus at rest,
Jocasta has told him about the oracle given to Laius that seemed not
to have been fulfilled. But the mention of the place where three highways met rouses a dreadful apprehension in the king's mind, and
at last he tells her the story of his encounter at just such a place.
If there is any connection (so he puts it, euphemistically) between
the old stranger he killed and Laius, who could be more wretched,
of a more hostile daimon (τίς ἐχθροδαίμων μᾶλλον; 816), than he now
is; for he is liable to his own ban pronounced upon the killer of
Laius, and he is sleeping with the wife of the man he killed. Not
only so, but he is in exile (so he thinks) from his native land for fear
of wedding his mother and killing his father. "Would not a man be
right to judge of me that these things come from a cruel daimon"
(ἀπ' ὠμοῦ . . . δαίμονος, 828). Oedipus, then, attributes to a cruel and
hostile superhuman power the destiny which is so much worse than
he yet knows. When it becomes known, when Oedipus, knowing it,
has entered the palace, the Chorus argue the nothingness of man
from the daimon of Oedipus.

Later in the ode they sing (1213 f.): "All-seeing time has found
you out (ἄκοντα); it brings to justice the monstrous marriage in which
the begotten has long been the begetter." This inadequate translation of the untranslatable omits one word: "unwilling" or "unwitting" as the epithet of Oedipus. The conscious criminal seeks to evade
detection, which comes upon him against his will. But this does not
apply. What, then, was contrary to the will or knowledge of Oedipus?
There is perhaps at this point a deliberate ambiguity,[3] which is
cleared up, when, a few lines later, a servant comes out of the palace,
now polluted (as he says) with new evils which will soon come to
light—"evils wrought consciously and not unwittingly" (ἑκόντα κοὐκ
ἄκοντα, 1230). A distinction could not more clearly and emphatically
be made between the unwilled and the willed deeds of Oedipus; and
it is reinforced by the Messenger's general comment, that "those
griefs sting most that are seen to be self-chosen" (αὐθαίρετοι, 1231).
The distinction is clearly made, and we expect it to be clearly main-

---

[3] "He had not foreseen the disclosure which was to result from his inquiry into
the murder of Laius" (Jebb) [Sir Richard C. Jebb, ed., Sophocles, The Plays and
Fragments, Part I, The Oedipus Tyrannus, 3rd ed. (Cambridge, 1902), ad loc.—
Editor's note]; he had not known that his actions were crimes. Cf. also O.C. 977,
987.

tained. When he killed his father and wedded his mother, Oedipus was a victim of the gods, but, when he blinded himself, he was a free agent. How attractive to look at matters in this way, and how limited the truth of it may be!

The messenger tells his story of the suicide of Jocasta and the self-blinding of Oedipus. The doors open again, and the blinded Oedipus comes out. The reactions of the Chorus are governed, as those of any audience must be, by this sight, the most dreadful they have ever seen. "What madness came upon you? Who was the *daimon* that leapt, with a bound exceeding the extreme, upon . . . ?" [4] Upon what? The whole expression is, once more, essentially untranslatable, but Jebb's translation here seems to miss the point and, above all, the relationship of these lines to the preceding choral ode. I can only conclude with a free expansion: ". . . upon that *moira* of yours that was already a *daimon's* evil work." The evil destiny of Oedipus had seemed to have reached an extreme point and to have provided the perfect paradigm of ill-starred humanity, but there was still a further point of misery to be reached, and that too is ascribed to the assault of a *daimon*. A few lines later, groping in his sightlessness, hearing his voice "borne from him on the air in a direction over which he has no control," [5] Oedipus exclaims: "Oh *Daimon*, that you should have sprung so far!" (ἰὼ δαῖμον, ἵν' ἐξήλου, 1311). It is clear from his preceding words and from the response of the Chorus that he is thinking of his blindness. Later again, the Chorus ask: "How could you bring yourself so to destroy your sight? What *daimon* moved you to it?" (τίς σ' ἐπῆρε δαιμόνων; 1328). Oedipus might have said—and critics sometimes write as though he had said: "As to my other sufferings[6] they were the work of Apollo, but, when I struck my eyes, the responsibility was mine alone (and you are wrong to ask what *daimon* moved me)." Actually he replies: "It was Apollo, my friends, it was Apollo that was bringing these sufferings of mine to completion. But it was none other's hand that struck the blow: it was I." [7] The reiterated name of Apollo must answer the question: "What *daimon?*" The expression "these sufferings of mine" cannot exclude and may primarily denote the visible suffering which domi-

----

[4]   τίς σ', ὦ τλᾶμον,
προσέβη μανία; τίς ὁ πηδήσας
μείζονα δαίμων τῶν μακίστων
πρὸς σῇ δυσδαίμονι μοίρᾳ;   (1299–1302)
[5] Jebb, on 1310.
[6] As though it were τὰ μὲν ἄλλα...
[7] 'Απόλλων τάδ' ἦν, 'Απόλλων, φίλοι,
ὁ κακὰ κακὰ τελῶν ἐμὰ τάδ' ἐμὰ πάθεα.
ἔπαισε δ' αὐτόχειρ νιν οὔ-
τις, ἀλλ' ἐγὼ τλάμων.   (1329–32)

nates the scene. It would be tidy to suppose that, while Apollo was responsible, through his oracle, for the earlier sufferings of Oedipus, the self-binding was an act of independent will unmotivated by divine power. But that is not how it is seen by either Oedipus or the Chorus.

What then, we may well ask, has now become of the clear distinction between involuntary and voluntary acts with which Sophocles introduced the scene? What, for that matter, has become of the unconsidering Sophocles? Surely here is a mind at work upon a train of thought—working with the formality traditional in Greek literary art in a verbal technique reminiscent of Aeschylus. (Might it not be suggested that, if thought imposes form, equally a poet who works with certain formal methods is almost forced to think?) It was a mind surely, not unaware of what contemporary minds were thinking. The thought has links with Homer and Aeschylus, but also with Socrates and Euripides. If the play was written in the early 420's (which is as good a guess as any), Socrates may already have been preaching that "no man errs wittingly"; and, since the self-blinding of Oedipus was the error of a mind clouded by passion, Socrates might have argued that it was not properly a witting or willing act.[8] Euripides, according to Snell,[9] controverted this Socratic doctrine in the *Hippolytus* of 428. This may or may not be true. Euripides, who about this time was writing tragedies of passion, may have been a purely humanistic psychologist or may have believed that irrational passions were external forces of a daemonic character.[10] It is at least clear that the nature and origin of passion was a living issue about the time when the *Oedipus Tyrannus* was written.

When I ask what has become of the clear distinction between involuntary and voluntary acts, I do not wish to imply that it has disappeared, but merely that it has been made to appear in a new light. The distinction has not disappeared, but both kinds of acts have been drawn within the ambit of the operation of *daimones*. What, then, did Sophocles mean, when he represented the "evils wrought wittingly," the "self-chosen grief," as the work of a *daimon*, as the work of Apollo? We can perhaps find the answer in two directions. The self-blinding of Oedipus was, as Socrates might have called it, a mistake. The Chorus think that it was the result of an

[8] The relationship between action (δράσας, 1327; αὐτόχειρ, 1331) and passion (πάθεα) is a subtle one—and τλήμων can carry both suggestions. In the *Coloneus* Oedipus, looking back, can say (266 f.): τά γ' ἔργα μου/πεπονθότ' ἐστὶ μᾶλλον ἢ δεδρακότα [my deeds were suffered more than they were acted].

[9] B. Snell, *Philologus*, 97 (1948), 125 ff.

[10] This question bulked large in the discussions at the Fondation Hardt in 1958. Cf. *Entretiens*, VI, esp. 73 ff.—the discussion of A. Rivier's paper. I would suggest that Euripides was a poet caught uneasily between two worlds and only at his greatest when he comes closest to the archaic world-view.

onset of madness. They ask what *daimon* brought him to it; and the word they use (ἐπαίρειν) is appropriate to a transport of emotion. It is true that Oedipus, like a Greek,[11] gives a reason: "What needed I to see?" But we cannot suppose that he struck his eyes on a purely rational consideration. And the argument progressively breaks down, as it becomes clear that all he has done is to lock himself in a dark prison with the memories of the past.[12] Now, to see in an emotional impulse the work of a *daimon* or god is Homeric; it is Aeschylean; it is a view which may even have left traces in Euripides. But this ascription of the self-blinding to a *daimon* is also part of the whole fabric of the play. By identifying the *daimon* with Apollo, Oedipus links his witting and unwitting acts, so that the self-blinding appears as the culmination of the evil destiny that has attended him since birth. It has often been pointed out—by no one more cogently than by Kitto[13]—that the divinely-appointed destiny of Oedipus comes about largely through actions on his part which spring directly from his character: it was *like* Oedipus that he must leave Corinth to discover the truth about his birth; it was *like* Oedipus to pursue his judicial enquiries with such energy; and so on. ἦθος ἀνθρώπῳ δαίμων: character is destiny. Looked at from this angle, the play might seem to be a commentary on the saying of Heraclitus. Yet, when, still acting characteristically, Oedipus blinds himself, the action is attributed to the influence of a *daimon*—and Heraclitus is turned inside out. There is a kind of symmetry. It needed the unwitting characteristic actions of Oedipus to bring about his fated destiny; it needed the influence of a *daimon* to explain his deliberate act. The divine and human worlds inter-penetrate; and this inter-penetration is Homeric and archaic.

*   *   *

The archaic is now fashionable in art, but in the realm of thought the word is still used as a term of disparagement. I would suggest that, under the pervasive influence of centuries of Platonic and

---

[11] And a character in a Greek tragedy. R. W. Livingstone, in *Greek Poetry and Life*, 160 f., and B. M. W. Knox, *Oedipus at Thebes*, 185 ff., seem to exaggerate the rationality of his action. 1271 ff. express an instinctive revulsion (upon which he acts with characteristic impetuosity); 1369 ff. are a rationalization, which is then shown to be illusory (see n. 2 below). This criticism does not of course affect the value of Knox's remarks about "the recovery of Oedipus" (op. cit. 185).

[12] The illusion of 1389–90 (τὸ γὰρ τὴν φροντίδ᾽ ἔξω τῶν κακῶν οἰκεῖν γλυκύ) [for it is sweet when one's thoughts dwell apart from one's troubles] is immediately dispelled, as Oedipus reviews his life, and above all by the vivid picture of 1398 f. Cf. 1401 (ἄρά μου μέμνησθ᾽ ἔτι . . . ;), but it is Oedipus who must live with this memory (cf. 1318).

[13] *Greek Tragedy*[3], 136 f.

Christian thinking, there is a tendency to undervalue the categories of archaic thought as a means of expressing important truths about the universe. There is an implicit criticism which I will put in so extreme and indeed absurd a form that it could not possibly be ascribed to any living scholar. Why, if Aeschylus and Sophocles were thinkers worthy of attention, did they not abandon the Urdummheit of the Archaic Age and become good Platonists before their time? It is true that, if they had enrolled proleptically under Plato's banner, they would not have been allowed to write tragedy, but this would have been no hardship, since, having once given their adherence to Plato, they would have lost both the will and the power to do so.

It is a sad—perhaps even a tragic—fact that advances in human thought tend to be bought at a price, which is the exchange of one set of difficulties for another. We have been concerned in particular with two related features of Greek archaic thought, which may or may not be its most salient characteristics, but are certainly those most relevant to tragedy. One of them might be called the involvement of the mind, the other the responsibility of the gods for evil.

The discovery of the mind (to use Snell's phrase), the disentanglement of the individual human personality, was vital to the development of morals and of civilization. Until the personality has been isolated, it cannot be valued; and it was not for nothing that Whitehead devoted an early chapter of *Adventures of Ideas* to the civilizing influence of the Platonic and Christian conceptions of the soul. Behind Plato is Socrates and the "tendance of the soul" ($\theta\epsilon\rho\alpha\pi\epsilon\acute{\iota}\alpha\ \psi\upsilon\chi\tilde{\eta}s$). But the soul cannot be tended, until it has been recognized; you cannot appeal to conscience except on the basis of the freedom of the will. This would seem pure gain. But then the danger appears. The autonomous will becomes an abstraction; the soul cuts loose from its connections with a body (becoming the ghost in the machine), from its connections with other souls and other bodies and with the totality of the universe. It is characteristic of much modern thought that it stresses the involvement of the human personality in its environment and the consequent limitations upon human freedom. The saying of Heraclitus, already quoted ($\mathring{\eta}\theta os\ \mathring{\alpha}\nu\theta\rho\acute{\omega}\pi\omega\ \delta\alpha\acute{\iota}\mu\omega\nu$), was, one supposes, a protest against superstition—and a fine one. But one problem it does not solve: it does not tell us where the *ethos* comes from. Syntactically reversible,[14] it yields as good a sense the other way round. It is doubtless a great advantage to be rid of superstitious fears and ideas of mechanical pollution and to get a clear juridical distinction between deliberate and unwitting actions. It may not be

---

[14] As this most oracular philosopher may conceivably have realized.

so good to forget that our deliberate acts are themselves in large measure the product of innumerable causes in the past over which we have no control. That is something that archaic thought was not tempted to forget—and that tragedy must never forget.

What the Greek poets expressed in terms of a mythology, we may express in psychological terms so little precise and so little understood that they have almost the status of a modern mythology.[15] We argue about free-will and determinism within a philosophical framework unknown to the Greek poets, but the debate is not exclusively a modern one. The Greeks loved liberty above all things and knew what it meant to be deprived of liberty. A slave-owning agricultural society presented obvious paradigms—metaphors which occur again and again in Greek tragedy. The free man follows his own choices; the slave and the yoked animal obey the bidding of a master; they are subject to compulsion (*ananke*). Feeling their liberty confined not only by external circumstances but even in the realm of their own minds, it was not surprising that the Greeks should ask themselves how far the free man was still free, in what degree he was constrained by the forces they conceived as gods. The question of psychological determination merges into the wider question of the responsibility of the gods for evil, which was such a rock of offence to Plato.

It was an offence that the tragedians—and he cites Aeschylus in particular—made the gods responsible for evil.[16] How far he really understood Aeschylus we cannot tell, but the better he understood him, the more the Plato of the *Republic* was bound to disapprove of him. The gods responsible for evil! But, if the gods are inside nature, as the Greeks' gods so obviously and so firmly were,[17] how can they not be responsible for evil? It was Plato's problem, not the tragedians'. It was Plato's problem how the gods could be made not to be so responsible. To put it rather crudely, the solution involved taking the gods out of nature and then trying to bring them back into it. If we look for the divine in Plato's thought, we find it, primarily, in a perfect world of Forms—and above all in the Form of the Good —to which the soul of man, itself divine, has access. It is, however, the rational soul that is divine and has such access; and we are left with the problem of irrational impulses and desires and the havoc they cause. In the *Timaeus* a divine demiurge is represented as making

---

[15] J. de Romilly (*Crainte et angoisse dans le théâtre d' Eschyle,* 104 f.) has some interesting remarks on the relationship between Aeschylus and modern psychological ideas.

[16] Plato, *Rep.* 379c–380c.

[17] "The Greek gods . . . were subordinate metaphysical entities, well within nature." A. N. Whitehead, *Science and the Modern World,* 202 (Pelican Books edition).

the world upon the model of the Forms; and, whether he is an external creator god or, as is more probable,[18] a mythical symbol of the Divine Reason working for good ends, we have to account for the manifold imperfections in the world he made. Plato, who on the whole speaks with such confidence and clarity in the *Republic,* was exercised—and, it would appear, increasingly exercised—by these problems. In the *Timaeus* he ascribes the imperfections of the craftsman's work to the imperfect tractability of the material (the metaphysical status of which remains rather obscure): he says[19]—and it is one of the most remarkable sayings in Plato—that "the generation of this universe was a mixed result of the combination of Necessity (*ananke*) and Reason." And he goes on: "Reason overruled Necessity by persuading her to guide the greatest part of the things that become towards what is best; in that way and on that principle this universe was fashioned in the beginning by the victory of reasonable persuasion over Necessity." Cornford, in an Epilogue to *Plato's Cosmology,* associated this passage with the closing scene of the *Eumenides*; and one would indeed like to think that Plato had taken Aeschylus to heart and that in this his most profound—perhaps his only profound—contribution to the problem of evil he links hands with Aeschylus and Sophocles—with Aeschylus who was pre-occupied with the successes, with Sophocles who was pre-occupied with the failures, of persuasion in the moral field.

But the *Timaeus* lies between the *Republic* and the *Laws.* It is not the hard sayings of the *Timaeus,* born of metaphysical perplexity, that have influenced subsequent thought and feeling so much as the ardent religious conviction and sheer literary power of the *Republic* and, particularly, the Myth of Er with which it closes. In this eschatological myth, souls are seen to choose their own destinies, but first they are addressed by a Prophetes, or Spokesman of the divine powers. His words are virtually a manifesto against the archaic—and the tragic—world-view. Though he speaks in the name of the Allotting Goddess (Lachesis), daughter of Necessity (Ananke), we find that lot affects only the order in which they choose and necessity only ratifies inflexibly their choice. "It is not," he says,[20] "that a *daimon* will get you by lot, but that you will choose a *daimon.* . . . Virtue owns no master. . . . The responsibility is the chooser's; God is not responsible." But in the *Laws* a disillusioned Plato has swung to the opposite extreme. Twice[21] he makes the Athenian speak contemptu-

---

[18] Cf. F. M. Cornford, *Plato's Cosmology,* 34 ff.

[19] 47e–48a (translated by Cornford).

[20] 617d–e. οὐχ ὑμᾶς δαίμων λήξεται, ἀλλ' ὑμεῖς δαίμονα αἱρήσεσθε . . . ἀρετὴ δὲ ἀδέσποτον . . . αἰτία ἐλομένου· θεὸς ἀναίτιος.

[21] 644d–e; cf. 803c–804b.

ously of men as puppets, playthings (perhaps) of the gods, jerked this way and that by their hopes and fears and passions, dancing on a string.

Such disillusionment is perhaps the nemesis that attends upon a too confident idealism. It is, however, no part of my purpose to deny such truth and value as may reside in the words of the Prophetes, but merely to suggest that neither puppets nor human-beings who are in complete control of their destinies can be the subjects of tragedy. The categories of archaic thought, primitive and obstructive though they might be in primitive minds, allowed Aeschylus and Sophocles to write tragedy, because—ascribe it to inferior logic or superior insight—they were able simultaneously to see man as free and as subject to determining powers, and so to produce that tension between freedom and necessity which seems essential to the tragic paradox. At least it can be said that, because of their archaic notions, and the presuppositions on which they were based, they were not tempted, as so many thinkers have been, to fudge the evidence in the interests of the autonomy of the will and the innocence of heaven.

The Last Scene

by Bernard M. W. Knox

But the play does not end with the proof of divine omniscience and human ignorance. It ends, as it begins, with Oedipus. "Equal to zero"—the chorus' estimate, proposed at the moment when Oedipus learns who he is, seems right and indeed inevitable. But it is hard to accept. It means that the heroic action of Oedipus, with all that his action is made to represent, is a hollow mockery, a snare and a delusion. It suggests that man should not seek, for fear of what he will find. It renounces the qualities and actions which distinguish man from the beasts, and accepts a state of blind, mute acquiescence no less repugnant to the human spirit than the recklessness demanded by Jocasta's universe of chance. And yet at that moment it seems the only possible conclusion. With Oedipus as their paradigm, it is difficult to see what other estimate the chorus can make.

A different estimate is proposed, not in words but in dramatic action, by the final scene of the play. For Oedipus, the paradigm, on whom the chorus' despairing estimate is based, surmounts the catastrophe and reasserts himself. He is so far from being equal to zero that in the last lines of the play[1] Creon has to tell him not to try to "rule in everything" (1522). This last scene of the play, so often criticized as

"The Last Scene" (editor's title) by Bernard M. W. Knox. From Chapter Five, "Hero," in Oedipus at Thebes (New Haven: Yale University Press, 1957), pp. 185–96, 265–66. Copyright © 1957 by Yale University Press. Reprinted by permission of the publisher.

[1] With Pearson and many others, I cannot believe that the play ended with the tasteless and hardly intelligible tetrameters of 1524–30. As the scholiast says (on 1523): καὶ αὐτάρκως ἔχει τὸ δρᾶμα· τὰ γὰρ ἑξῆς ἀνοίκεια γνωμολογοῦντος Οἰδίποδος. By which he meant, I take it, that these lines are inappropriate for Oedipus (and in fact all the MSS attribute them to the chorus) and impossible for the chorus (which could hardly say ὦ πάτρας Θήβης ἔνοικοι, words which are possible only if the chorus does not consist of Thebans, like the chorus of the Euripidean Phoenissae). Apart from this obvious indication that these miserable lines were written for the end of the Phoenissae (whether Euripides wrote them is another question), the plural αἰνίγματα in 1525 is meaningless, and 1526 and the last three lines defy sense and syntax alike.

anticlimactic or unbearable, is on the contrary vital for the play, and
a development which makes its acceptance possible. It shows us the
recovery of Oedipus, the reintegration of the hero, the reconstitution
of the imperious, dynamic, intelligent figure of the opening scenes.

This is an astonishing development, for Oedipus, when he comes
out of the palace, is so terrible a sight that the chorus cannot bear to
look at him (1303), and his situation is such that the chorus expresses
a wish that it had never known him (1348). It approves his wish that
he could have died on the mountainside before he reached manhood
(1356), and tells him that he would be better dead now than alive
and blind (1368). This despair is reflected in the words of Oedipus
himself: they are the words of a broken man.

The first lines present us with an Oedipus who speaks in terms we
can hardly recognize: he speaks of his movements, voice, and destiny
as things alien to him, utterly beyond his control. "Where am I being
carried? How does my voice fly about, carried aloft? O my destiny,
to what point have you leaped out?" (1309–11).[2] These are the words
of a blinded man awakening to the realization of his terrible impo-
tence, but they express also a feeling that Oedipus is no longer an
active force but purely passive. This impression is enforced by his
next words, an address to the darkness in which he will now forever
move, and a reference to the pain which pierces his eyes and mind
alike (1313–18). The climax of this unnatural passivity is reached
when Oedipus first becomes aware of the presence of the chorus
(1321). His realization takes the form of a grateful recognition of their
steadfastness in "looking after the blind man" (1323). This is an expression of his utter dependency on others; he is so far from action now
that he needs help even to exist. He seems indeed a zero, equal to
nothing.

It is precisely at this point that the chorus reminds us, and him,
that part at any rate of his present calamitous state, his blindness,
is his own choice, the result of his own independent action after the
recognition of the truth. This was not called for by the prophecy of
Apollo, nor was it demanded in the oracle's instructions about the
murderer's punishment or the curse on him pronounced by Oedipus.
It was Oedipus' autonomous action, and the chorus now asks him
why he did it: "You have done dreadful things" (*deina drasas*, 1327).
They use the word for action which was peculiarly his when he was
tyrannos, and the question they ask him suggests an explanation.
"Which of the divinities spurred you on?" Oedipus' reply defends

<hr/>

[2] φέρομαι and φοράδην. For φοράδην see Jebb's note: "in the manner of that
which is carried." Jebb comments: "He feels as if his voice was borne from him on
the air in a direction over which he has no control."

his action and rejects the chorus' formula, which would shift the responsibility for the blinding off his shoulders. Apollo, he says, brought my sufferings to fulfilment, but "as for the hand that struck my eyes, it was mine and no one else's" (1330–31). He confirms what the messenger has already told us; the action was "self-chosen" (*authairetoi,* 1231), and a few lines later the chorus reproves him for it. It was in fact an action typical of Oedipus *tyrannos,* one which anticipated the reaction, advice, and objection of others, a *fait accompli,* a swift decisive act for which he assumes full responsibility and which he proceeds to defend. And now, as if the chorus' reminder of his own action had arrested the disintegration of his personality which was so terribly clear in the first speech after his entrance, the old Oedipus reappears. As he rejects the chorus' suggestion that the responsibility was not his, grounds his action logically, and (as his lines make the transition from the lyric of lamentation to the iambic of rational speech), rejects their reproaches, all the traits of his magnificent character reappear. It is not long before he is recognizably the same man as before.

He is still the man of decisive action, and still displays the courage which had always inspired that action. His attitude to the new and terrible situation in which he now finds himself is full of the same courage which he displayed before: he accepts the full consequences of the curse he imposed on himself, and insists stubbornly, in the face of Creon's opposition, that he be put to death or exiled from Thebes. He brushes aside the compromise offered by Creon with the same courage that dismissed the attempts of Tiresias, Jocasta, and the herdsman to stop the investigation. The speed and impatience of his will is if anything increased; *tachys,* "swift," is still his word. "Take me away from this place as quickly as possible" (*hoti tachista,* 1340). "Hide me away as quickly as possible" (*hopôs tachista,* 1410). "Throw me out of this land as quickly as may be" (*hoson tachisth',* 1436).

As before, he has no patience with half-measures or delay; the oracle and his own curse call for his exile or death, and he sees nothing to be gained by prolonging the inaction. The same analytical intelligence is at work; he is right, and, as we know, Creon finally does late what Oedipus wanted done early—he exiles Oedipus from Thebes. The same hard intelligence which insisted on full clarity and all the facts is displayed in his remorseless exploration and formulation of the frightful situation in which he finds himself. He spares himself no detail of the consequences of his pollution for himself and for his daughters. It is typical that while Creon's reaction is to cover and conceal (1426 ff.), Oedipus brings everything out into the open, analyzing in painful detail his own situation and that of his children. The intelligence of Oedipus is at work even at the high pitch of semihysterical grief;[3] even in his outburst of lamentation he distinguishes between what he regards as the gods' responsibility and his own. And an extraordinary thing emerges as Oedipus abandons the wild lament of his first reaction for the reasoned speech of the last part of the play: it becomes apparent that even the self-blinding was based on the deliberation and reflection which in Oedipus *tyrannos* always preceded action.[4] To the chorus' reproach that he had "made a bad decision" (1367) in blinding himself he replies with the old impatience and a touch of the old anger. "Do not read me a lesson or give me any advice, to the effect that I have not done the best thing" (1369–70). And he goes on to describe in detail the reasoning by which he arrived at the decision to put out his eyes (1370–83). Sophocles makes it clear that this is an account of past reflection preceding the action (and not a present rationalization of it) by his use of the past tense throughout the speech.[5] Oedipus is fully confident of the rightness of the action and the thought which preceded and produced it. And all through this scene he maps out the future for himself and his family, giving Creon instructions for the burial of Jocasta, his own expulsion from Thebes, and the upbringing of his sons and daughters.

The old confidence in his own intelligence and action is still there, but the exaggerated and vaulting hopefulness is gone. And yet there is still a kind of hope; he becomes certain, after his initial wish for death, that he is destined to live, that he is in some sense indestructible. "This much I know [*oida*]: that not disease, nor anything else can destroy me. For I would never have been saved from death in the first place [i.e. as a child on the mountainside] except for some strange and fearful evil" (*deinôi kakôi*, 1457). He feels himself as eminent in disaster as he once was in prosperity—"my sufferings are such as no one could bear but me" (1414–15); whatever his end will be, it will be out of the ordinary, like everything else about him. "But let my destiny go, wherever it is going" (1458).

The devotion to the interests of the city which was so marked a feature of the attitude of the *tyrannos* might be expected to become dormant in the man who is now a polluted outcast from society, but on the contrary it is still active in Oedipus. His anxiety to have the terms of his own curse and the command of the oracle exactly and

---

[3] For which the medium is the lyric meter of his opening song after his reappearance on stage: he does not return to the iambic medium of rational speech until he begins to argue in 1369.

[4] For the blinding as "deliberate purpose" see Sir Richard Livingstone, "The Exodos of the *Oedipus Tyrannus*," in *Greek Poetry and Life* (Oxford, 1936), p. 160.

[5] ἂν προσεῖδον, 1372; ὄψις ἦν, 1375; ἔμελλον . . . ὁρᾶν, 1385. What Oedipus says now about what he thought then is proved exact by the messenger's account of what he said at the time (1271–74).

immediately fulfilled springs partly from his sense of the city's need of release from the plague, which can come only through the punishment of the murderer of Laius. It is in terms of the interest of the city that he states his desire for exile, speaking this time not as *tyrannos* but with a consciousness of his newly revealed position as the hereditary monarch: "Let not the city of my fathers be condemned to have me as a living inhabitant" (1449–50).

And Oedipus is still adaptable, quick to align himself with changed circumstances. The process of his swift adjustment to his blindness is carefully delineated. After the helpless desperation of the opening lines, in which he is oblivious of any reality outside himself, he comes to realize that he has still some power of perception and recognition —he can hear. "You are not unperceived," he tells the chorus; "I distinguish clearly [*gignôskô saphôs*, 1325] your voice at any rate, plunged in darkness though I am." And from the point at which he recognizes the possibilities as well as the limitations of his new state, he never turns back. He begins to adapt himself to the larger aspects of the situation, and makes the transition from passive back to active.

The adaptability of Oedipus surmounts the most terrible reversal of relationships imaginable. Oedipus is now an outcast, and, as Tiresias told him he would be, a beggar. The wealthy *tyrannos* expressed his wish as an order, but the beggar lives by insistent appeals, by emphatic and often importunate pleading. When Creon appears, Oedipus shows himself to be as insistent a beggar as ever lived; the formulas of supplication come as easily from his lips as the imperative words, and they are charged with the same fierce energy. Once Oedipus is told that Creon has not come to mock him, he shows himself an adept in his new role; appeal and entreaty follow each other swiftly —Creon is given no breathing space. "By the gods . . . do what I ask," he says (1432), begging to be expelled from the city, and Creon recognizes the tone of his speech, for he replies "You importune me" (*lipareis*, 1435), the appropriate word for the action of the beggar. In the subsequent appeal to be allowed the privilege of saying farewell to his children, Oedipus achieves a wheedling importunacy which is formally emphasized by the breaks in the regularity of the verses: 1468, 1471, and 1475 are cut off short before the end of the first measure. "Let me touch them, and weep for their sorrows. Grant it, my lord. Grant it, you who are noble in birth." This last phrase is a reference to his own polluted fatherhood; it is the beggar's characteristic contrast between the nobility of his patron's birth and the humble nature of his own circumstances. Oedipus greets the granting of his request with the beggar's typical blessing of his benefactor—"May you be fortunate . . ." (1478)—and the same flattering contrast of circumstances—"May a divinity prove a better guardian to you than it did

to me" (1479). Later he makes another appeal to Creon's pity, this
time on behalf of his daughters: "Do not let them wander husband-
less as beggars, do not make their fortune the equivalent of mine"
(1505–7)—a phrase which indicates his conception of his own status
as a beggar. "Pity them," he continues (1508); "Nod your head in
sign of acceptance, noble man, touch them with your hand" (1510).
Oedipus has made a swift and strikingly successful adjustment to his
new role. As a beggar he is irresistible.[6]

For this abject and insistent supplication is full of an imperiousness
that recalls the *tyrannos*. When he first hears the voice of Creon, whom
he had wrongly condemned to death, he is abashed and at a loss for
words (1419), yet in a few moments he is arguing stubbornly with
him, and finally gives him his instructions in a magnificent phrase
which combines the attitude of the *tyrannos* and the beggar: "I make
you responsible and I beg you . . ." (*episkêptô te kai prostrepsomai*,
1446). The first word is the same one which he used before, when as
tyrannos he ordered the people of Thebes to cooperate with him in
his search for the murderer of Laius.

It is a surprising word, and even more surprising is the fact that
Creon does not protest. The last scene of the play presents us with
an unpredictable situation: in spite of his tremendous reversal, Oedipus is still the active force which binds men and circumstances to
its will. His reflection and intelligence assure him that he must go
immediately into exile, and to this point of view he clings stubbornly,
urging it persistently and imperiously on Creon until the man who
now has the power to "decide and act" (1417) yields to the will of the
blind beggar. At the last moment, when Creon orders him into the
house, Oedipus imposes conditions (1517); the conditions are the
same demand he has so stubbornly repeated throughout the scene—
that Creon immediately exile him from Thebes (1518). Creon's attempt
to shift the responsibility by consulting Delphi is rejected by Oedipus,
and he is right; according to the original oracular advice, and also
the curse pronounced by Oedipus, the murderer of Laius must be
exiled. "I come as one most hateful to the gods," says Oedipus (1519).
Creon yields to his demands, but in an ambiguous phrase: "For that
reason you will swiftly get what you want" (1519)—which might mean
either "I will exile you" or "the gods, since they hate you, will,

---

[6] The beggar is shameless in his importunity (κακὸς δ᾽ αἰδοῖος ἀλήτης, says Penelope,
Od. xvii. 578, "a modest beggar is no good"); he compliments the man he hopes to
make his patron (Odysseus to Antinous, ibid., 415 ff.); he compares his own
miserable circumstances with the splendid prosperity of his patron (ibid. 419 ff.);
he calls down blessings on his benefactor's head (Odysseus to Eumaeus, *Od.* xiv.
53–54). Cf. also xvii. 354–55. All these formulas of the beggar are to be found in
Oedipus' appeals to Creon.

through the agency of the oracle, command your banishment." Oedipus demands a clear promise: "You consent, then?" (1520). And Creon finally does consent, and though the terms of his consent are still ambiguous they commit him much more strongly than his previous statement. "It is not my custom to say idly what I do not think" (1520).[7] It is a phrase worthy of Creon the politician, but Oedipus accepts it as a definite promise, and allows himself to be led into the palace. Before he does, he makes an attempt to take the children with him, but at this point Creon finally asserts himself and separates the children from their father. He takes the occasion to reprove Oedipus for his imperious tone. "Do not wish to exercise power [*kratein*, 1522] in everything. For the power which you won [*hakratêsas*, 1522] has not accompanied you to the end of your life." He does not get his way in everything, but in most he has, including the most important issue of all, his expulsion; in this the blind beggar has imposed his will on the king.

The final phrase of Creon—"Do not wish to exercise power in everything"—brings us full circle; it is an echo of the first words addressed to Oedipus in the play; "Oedipus, you who exercise power in my country," the priest said to him at the beginning (*kratynôn*, 14). Creon actually has to remind the blinded polluted man that he is no longer *tyrannos;* the will of Oedipus is reasserting itself, and Creon suddenly sees that "action and deliberation," the functions which he assumed when Oedipus was revealed as the son of Laius, are slipping from him. The swiftness and force of Oedipus' recovery from the shock of self-recognition can be gauged from the fact that in the very last line of the play Oedipus has to be reminded of his reversal.

This recovery is all the more astonishing because there is no reference in Sophocles' lines to the justification of Oedipus and his elevation to the status of divine hero which is the subject of the later play *Oedipus at Colonus.*[8] There is, at most, a sense that Oedipus has a special destiny, an invulnerability to ordinary calamities, but this

---

[7] See Jebb's note. The expression is completely ambiguous, for φρονῶ can mean either "understanding" (i.e. "I do not idly speak things I do not understand—and will not understand until I consult the oracle again") or "intention" (in which case it is a definite concession to Oedipus). Yet Jebb is surely right in taking it in the latter sense (as Oedipus evidently does), and there is then no contradiction between this passage and the reference to Oedipus' exile in *O.C.* 765 ff. From the *O.C.* it appears that Creon never did, in fact, consult the oracle of Apollo about the exile of Oedipus; the decision to exile him was made by Creon alone and connived at by Oedipus' sons. The words οὐκ ἤθελες, *O. C.* 767, mean not "refused" but simply "were unwilling," as Creon in the *Oedipus Tyrannus* clearly is.

[8] See "Sophocles' Oedipus," in *Tragic Themes in Western Literature,* ed. Cleanth Brooks (New Haven, 1955), pp. 23–29.

special destiny Oedipus can only refer to as a "dreadful evil" (*deinôi kakôi*, 1457). The reassertion of Oedipus' forceful personality rests on no change in his situation, no promise or assurance, human or divine; it is, like every one of his actions and attitudes, autonomous, the expression of a great personality which defies human expectation as it once defied divine prophecy.

The closing note of the tragedy is a renewed insistence on the heroic nature of Oedipus; the play ends as it began, with the greatness of the hero. But it is a different kind of greatness. It is now based on knowledge, not, as before, on ignorance,[9] and this new knowledge is, like that of Socrates, a recognition of man's ignorance. "Apollo and Zeus," the chorus sang, "have understanding and knowledge of things human" (497–99); and Oedipus now directs the full force of his intelligence and action to the fulfilment of the oracular command that the murderer of Laius be killed or exiled. Creon, who resists the appeals of Oedipus, can taunt him with his former lack of belief—"You would have faith in the god now" (1445)—but Oedipus does not deign to answer this sarcastic rebuke. He hammers away insistently at his demand that the command of the oracle be literally and immediately fulfilled. The heroic qualities of the *tyrannos,* once exercised against prophecy and the destiny of which it is the expression, are now ranged on its side. And Creon's refusal to fulfil the oracle's command presents us with a situation in which Oedipus' acceptance of what he once rejected demands and produces not passivity but action, not acquiescence but struggle. The heroic qualities of Oedipus are still to be given full play, but now with, not against, the powers that shape destiny and govern the world. "May Destiny be with me . . ." the chorus sang when it abandoned Oedipus (863); that prayer is fulfilled for the hero. Destiny is with him; the confidence which was once based solely on himself is now more firmly based; it proceeds now from a knowledge of the nature of reality and the forces which govern it, and his identification with their will. In the last scene he champions the command of the oracle against the will of Creon, the new ruler of Thebes; it is Creon now who displays a politic attitude towards the Delphic oracle, and Oedipus who insists on its literal fulfilment. He is now blind like Tiresias, and like Tiresias has a more penetrating vision than the ruler he opposes; in this scene he has in fact become the spokesman of Apollo, "seeing," as the chorus said of Tiresias, "the same things as the lord Apollo." Now that his will is identified with *moira,* "destiny," his action ceases to be self-defeating, for it is based

---

[9] D. Chr. lxiv. 6 says, of Oedipus: ἡ τύχη γὰρ αὐτῷ τὸ μηδὲν παθεῖν περιποιουμένη τὸ ἀγνοεῖν ἔδωκεν, ὅπερ ὅμοιον ἦν τῷ μὴ παθεῖν. εἶτα ἅμα τῆς εὐτυχίας ἐπαύσατο καὶ τοῦ γιγνώσκειν ἤρξατο.

on true knowledge. The greatness of Oedipus in his ruin is no less, and in some senses more, than the greatness of the *tyrannos*.

Oedipus is a paradigm of all mankind, and of the city which is man's greatest creation. His resurgence in the last scene of the play is a prophetic vision of a defeated Athens which will rise to a greatness beyond anything she had attained in victory, a vision of man, superior to the tragic reversal of his action and the terrible success of his search for truth, reasserting his greatness, not this time in defiance of the powers which shape human life but in harmony with those powers. "All things are born to be diminished," Pericles reminded the Athenians; the tragic vision of Sophocles accepts this melancholy recognition and transcends it, to see beyond the defeat of man's ambition the true greatness of which only the defeated are capable.

The *Oedipus Tyrannus* of Sophocles combines two apparently irreconcilable themes, the greatness of the gods and the greatness of man, and the combination of these themes is inevitably tragic, for the greatness of the gods is most clearly and powerfully demonstrated by man's defeat. "The god is great in his laws and he does not grow old." But man does, and not only does he grow old, he also dies. Unlike the gods, he exists in time. The beauty and power of his physical frame is subject to sickness, death, and corruption; the beauty and power of his intellectual, artistic, and social achievement to decline, overthrow, and oblivion. His greatness and beauty arouse in us a pride in their magnificence which is inseparable from and increased by our sorrow over their immanent and imminent death. Oedipus is symbolic of all human achievement: his hard-won magnificence, unlike the everlasting magnificence of the divine, cannot last, and while it lives, shines all the more brilliant against the somber background of its impermanency. Sophocles' tragedy presents us with a terrible affirmation of man's subordinate position in the universe, and at the same time with a heroic vision of man's victory in defeat. Man is not equated to the gods, but man at his greatest, as in Oedipus, is capable of something which the gods, by definition, cannot experience; the proud tragic view of Sophocles sees in the fragility and inevitable defeat of human greatness the possibility of a purely human heroism to which the gods can never attain, for the condition of their existence is everlasting victory.

PART TWO

View Points

Plutarch

Curiosity involved Oedipus in the greatest misfortunes. For it was while inquiring into his own identity, in the belief that he was not a Corinthian but a foreigner, that he met Laius. And when he had killed Laius and won the throne and taken his mother to wife as well, and was to all appearances a fortunate man, he once more made inquiry into his identity. And though his wife tried to stop him, he grew all the more insistent in questioning the old man who knew the facts, bringing every compulsion to bear. Finally, when the affair was already bringing him round to a suspicion of the truth and the old man had cried out, "Alas! I am on the very point of saying the fearful thing!" Oedipus, inflamed by his affliction and in a spasm of excitement, nonetheless answered, "And I of hearing it. But all the same it must be heard." So it is that the itch of curiosity is a sweetly bitter, uncontrollable thing. . . .

(On Curiosity 522bc, trans. M. J. O'B.)

"Longinus"

In lyric poetry would you choose to be Bacchylides rather than Pindar, and in tragedy Ion of Chios rather than (heaven help us!) Sophocles? These, to be sure, are faultless and altogether fine writers of the polished style, whereas Pindar and Sophocles, who at times, one might say, set fire to everything in their flight, are often unaccountably quenched and collapse disastrously. But would any sensible man who had collected and lined up the works of Ion judge them fair compensation for the single drama *Oedipus*?

(On the Sublime 33.5, trans. M. J. O'B.)

Voltaire

It is already contrary to probability that Oedipus, who has reigned for such a long time, should not know how his predecessor died. But that he should not even know whether it was in the country or in the city that this murder was committed, and that he should not give the slightest reason or the slightest excuse for his ignorance—I confess that I know of no word to express such an absurdity.

It is, one might say, a fault of the subject and not of the author; as if it were not up to the author to correct his subject when it is defective!

*   *   *

But what is still more astonishing, or rather what is not astonishing at all after such offenses against probability, is that Oedipus, when he learns that Phorbas [i.e. the Theban herdsman] is still alive, does not dream of simply having him sought out; he amuses himself by pronouncing curses and consulting oracles, without commanding that the only man who could enlighten him be brought before him. The chorus itself, which is so intent on seeing an end to the misfortunes of Thebes, and which gives Oedipus constant advice, does not advise him to question this witness to the death of the late king; it asks him only to send for Teiresias.

(From the *Third Letter on Oedipus*, trans. M. J. O'B.)

J. G. (Sir James) Frazer

Among many savage races breaches of the marriage laws are thought to blast the fruits of the earth through excessive rain or excessive drought. Similar notions of the disastrous effects of sexual crimes may be detected among some of the civilised races of antiquity, who seem not to have limited the supposed sterilising influence of such offences to the fruits of the earth, but to have extended it also to women and cattle. Thus among the Hebrews we read how Job, passionately protesting his innocence before God, declares that he is no adulterer; "For that," says he, "were an heinous crime; yea, it were an iniquity to be punished by the judges: for it is a fire that consumeth unto Destruction, and would root out all mine increase." [1] In this passage the Hebrew word translated "increase" commonly means "the produce of the earth;" and if we give the word its usual sense here, then Job

---

From J. G. Frazer, The Golden Bough, A Study in Magic and Religion, *3rd ed., Part I,* The Magic Art and the Evolution of Kings, *Vol. II (London: Macmillan & Co., Ltd., 1911), 113–15. Copyright 1911 by James George Frazer. Reprinted, with the omission of several footnotes, by permission of Trinity College, Cambridge, England.*

[1] Job xxxi. 11 *sq.* (Revised Version).

affirms adultery to be destructive of the fruits of the ground, which
is just what many savages still believe.

*   *   *

It would seem that the ancient Greeks and Romans entertained
similar notions as to the wasting effect of incest. According to Sophocles the land of Thebes suffered from blight, from pestilence, and
from the sterility both of women and of cattle under the reign of
Oedipus, who had unwittingly slain his father and wedded his mother,
and the Delphic oracle declared that the only way to restore the
prosperity of the country was to banish the sinner from it, as if his
mere presence withered plants, animals, and women. No doubt the
poet and his hearers set down these public calamities in great part
to the guilt of parricide, which rested on Oedipus; but they can hardly
have failed to lay much also of the evil at the door of his incest with
his mother.

Paul Shorey

I do not myself greatly care for the *Oedipus Tyrannus*. It moves
me on the stage, but in the closet my feeling about it is a little that of
Tolstoi towards *King Lear*. The original assumption, the *donnée,* is
too unreasonable, and this fairy-tale quality affects and infects the
plot. Aristotle's apology is that the irrationality is outside of and
precedes the main action. This reminds us of the dialogue between
Sneerwell and Puff in Sheridan's *Critic*: "Pray, Mr. Puff, how came
Sir Christopher Hatton never to ask that question before?" Puff:
"What! Before the play began? How the plague could he?"—"That's
true, in faith." The same point is made in *The Rehearsal*: "But
pray then, how comes it to pass that they know one another no better?"
—"That's for the better carrying on of the plot." That may serve as
an apology for Oedipus's ignorance of well-known facts about the
Thebes in which he had been king for years and about the former
husband of the woman he had married. But the fundamental folk-
lore or fairy-tale irrationality is irremediable. The Gallic wit and
light common sense of the French critic Lemaître hit the nail on the
head. The underlying thought is not to be taken seriously. It is
merely an answer to a primitive conundrum, What is the worst thing

From the lecture "Sophocles" by Paul Shorey, in Martin Classical Lectures, *I
(Cambridge, Mass.: Harvard University Press, 1931), 68–69. Copyright 1931 by the
Board of Trustees of Oberlin College. Reprinted by permission of the publisher.*

that could happen to a man? Why, to kill his father and marry his mother.

T. B. L. Webster

In the *Tyrannus* both Apollo and his ministers are triumphantly justified and the scepticism of Iocasta and Oedipus condemned. Sophocles is supporting the traditional religion against contemporary attacks. Criticism of oracles was particularly common at the time of the Peloponnesian war. False oracles were produced in large quantities, and the oracle-monger became a figure for the comic stage. Thucydides tells us that only one of the prophecies about the Peloponnesian war had come true, and Euripides in his *Philoctetes* (produced in 431) said that prophecy was a mere delusion. In this atmosphere Sophocles wrote the *Tyrannus* to defend what was for him, as for Socrates, one of the basic facts of religion.

From *T. B. L. Webster,* An Introduction to Sophocles (*Oxford: The Clarendon Press, 1936*), *p. 23. Copyright 1936 by the Clarendon Press. Reprinted by permission of the publisher.*

Werner Jaeger

Like Aeschylus, Sophocles thinks of drama as the instrument through which men reach a sublime knowledge. But it is not τὸ φρονεῖν, which was the ultimate certainty and necessity in which Aeschylus found peace. It is rather a tragical self-knowledge, the Delphic γνῶθι σεαυτόν deepened and broadened into a comprehension of the shadowy nothingness of human strength and human happiness. To know oneself is thus for Sophocles to know man's powerlessness; but it is also to know the indestructible and conquering majesty of suffering humanity. The agony of every Sophoclean character is an essential element in his nature. The strange fusion of character and fate is nowhere more movingly and mysteriously expressed than in the greatest of his heroes, to whom he returned once again at the very close of his life. It is Oedipus, a blind old man begging his way through the world, led by his daughter Antigone—another of Sophocles' most beloved

From *Werner Jaeger,* Paideia: The Ideals of Greek Culture, *trans. from the 2nd German ed. by Gilbert Highet, 4th English ed., I,* Archaic Greece, The Mind of Athens (*Oxford: Basil Blackwell & Mott Ltd., 1954*), *284. Copyright 1954 by Basil Blackwell & Mott Ltd. Reprinted by permission of the publisher.*

figures. Nothing reveals the essence of Sophoclean tragedy more deeply
than the fact that the poet grew old, as it were, along with his characters. He never forgot what Oedipus was to become. From the first,
the tragic king who was to bear the weight of the whole world's sufferings was an almost symbolic figure. He was suffering humanity
personified.

A. J. A. Waldock

Let us suppose that the hero is not just *Oedipus,* a mere man who
for inscrutable reasons has been picked out for special attention by
the gods. Let us suppose that he stands for something—"human suffering" will conveniently do. Let us also depersonalize the gods—treat
them a little abstractly by referring rather to the "universe of circumstance as it is." Immediately the play seems lifted; once more a
new dignity accrues. It is unnecessary to argue for a thesis, we need
not maintain that the play makes a point; but to have embodied
human suffering—there already is an achievement. To have given
dramatic expression to the universe of circumstance as it is—no
work accomplishing that could be thought of as destitute of content.

This is a neat manoeuvre, but . . . illegitimate. . . . It is just one
more way of smuggling significance into the *Oedipus Tyrannus;*
just one more expression of the feeling that this work, by hook or by
crook, must be made to mean something; just another attempt to
prove that the work really is universal. But the action of this play
is exceptional; no argument can alter that. Oedipus is a world-wonder
in his suffering, in his peculiar destiny he is a freak. He is a man
selected out of millions to undergo this staggering fate; that is why
his story is so fascinating. It fascinates because it is rare; because on
any rational assessment his story—as far as we are concerned—is
impossible. We can imagine it all so vividly, we can live in every
one of his emotions; yet we should as reasonably fear to be hit by a
thunderbolt as to be embroiled in his particular set of misfortunes.
And if Oedipus, by the extreme rarity of his destiny, is outside the
common lot of mankind, so is the special malignance that strikes him
a thing quite apart from the universe of circumstance as it is. Circumstance has its practical jokes and its sinister-seeming moods, but
a concatenation of malevolences on this scale is an absolutely unparal-

From A. J. A. Waldock, Sophocles the Dramatist *(Cambridge: Cambridge University Press, 1951), pp. 159–60. Copyright 1951 by Cambridge University Press.
Reprinted by permission of the publisher.*

leled thing. The gods who really do stand for circumstance are very much milder beings and need cause no great affright. That is why it is so misleading to reduce this play to the normal.

C. M. (Sir Maurice) Bowra

King Oedipus shows the humbling of a great and prosperous man by the gods. This humbling is not deserved; it is not a punishment for insolence, nor in the last resort is it due to any fault of judgement or character in the man. The gods display their power because they will. But since they display it, man may draw a salutary lesson. This is kept till the end of the play when the Chorus, or perhaps Oedipus himself, point to the extent of his fall, and comment:

> And, being mortal, think on that last day of death,
> Which all must see, and speak of no man's happiness
> Till, without sorrow, he hath passed the goal of life.

. . . After the hideous and harrowing events this finale of *King Oedipus* may seem a little tame. Yet it provides a quiet end, such as the Greeks liked, and it is Sophocles' conclusion on what has taken place.

From C. M. Bowra, Sophoclean Tragedy *(Oxford: The Clarendon Press, 1944), p. 175. Copyright 1944 by the Clarendon Press. Reprinted by permission of the publisher.*

Sigmund Freud

Now you will be impatiently waiting to hear what this terrible Oedipus complex comprises. The name tells you: you all know the Greek myth of King Oedipus, whose destiny it was to slay his father and to wed his mother, who did all in his power to avoid the fate prophesied by the oracle, and who in self-punishment blinded himself when he discovered that in ignorance he had committed both these crimes. I trust that many of you have yourselves experienced the profound effect of the tragic drama fashioned by Sophocles from this story. The Attic poet's work portrays the gradual discovery of the deed of Oedipus, long since accomplished, and brings it slowly to light by skillfully prolonged enquiry, constantly fed by new evidence; it has thus a certain resemblance to the course of a psycho-analysis. In the dia-

From Sigmund Freud, A General Introduction to Psychoanalysis, *trans. by Joan Riviere (New York: Liveright Publishing Corp., 1935), pp. 290–91. Copyright © 1963 by Joan Riviere. Reprinted with permission of Liveright Publishing Corp. and George Allen & Unwin, Ltd.*

logue the deluded mother-wife, Jocasta, resists the continuation of the enquiry; she points out that many people in their dreams have mated with their mothers, but that dreams are of no account. To us dreams are of much account, especially typical dreams which occur in many people; we have no doubt that the dream Jocasta speaks of is intimately related to the shocking and terrible story of the myth.

It is surprising that Sophocles' tragedy does not call forth indignant remonstrance in its audience. . . . For at bottom it is an immoral play; it sets aside the individual's responsibility to social law, and displays divine forces ordaining the crime and rendering powerless the moral instincts of the human being which would guard him against the crime. It would be easy to believe that an accusation against destiny and the gods was intended in the story of the myth; in the hands of the critical Euripides, at variance with the gods, it would probably have become such an accusation. But with the reverent Sophocles there is no question of such an intention; the pious subtlety which declares it the highest morality to bow to the will of the gods, even when they ordain a crime, helps him out of the difficulty. I do not believe that this moral is one of the virtues of the drama, but neither does it detract from its effect; it leaves the hearer indifferent; he does not react to this, but to the secret meaning and content of the myth itself. He reacts as though by self-analysis he had detected the Oedipus complex in himself, and had recognized the will of the gods and the oracle as glorified disguises of his own unconscious; as though he remembered in himself the wish to do away with his father and in his place to wed his mother, and must abhor the thought. The poet's words seem to him to mean: "In vain do you deny that you are accountable, in vain do you proclaim how you have striven against these evil designs. You are guilty, nevertheless; for you could not stifle them; they still survive unconsciously in you." And psychological truth is contained in this; even though man has repressed his evil desires into his Unconscious and would then gladly say to himself that he is no longer answerable for them, he is yet compelled to feel his responsibility in the form of a sense of guilt for which he can discern no foundation.

Thomas Gould

Could Sophocles himself have believed that Oedipus was a guiltless victim through and through? How could a man remain religious who

From Thomas Gould, "The Innocence of Oedipus: The Philosophers on Oedipus the King," *Part I,* Arion *IV (1965), 375–77. Copyright © 1965 by* Arion. *Reprinted by permission of* Arion.

had a vision like that? And how could a man be thought to be pious
by his fellow citizens when he presented them with plays containing
such a hopeless message?

But then it turns out that there are innumerable religious myths
that depend on this very point—guiltless suffering. Some mediaeval
Jews are said to have believed that God had given each generation
one just man, one man who not only suffered terribly through no fault
of his own, but knew that his suffering was not just. The misery of
this blameless man was thought somehow to lighten the burden for
the rest of mankind. The power of the *Book of Job,* also of *Prometheus Bound* and the latter plays of the *Oresteia,* also the *Ajax, Antigone, Hippolytus, Orestes, Hamlet, The Idiot, The Trial,* and many
other myths and stories, seems to require a similar consciousness of
innocence on the part of the sufferer.

And so we must face the larger question: why do stories of injustice
thrill good men? The Passion of Christ offers an illuminating if rather
special example. Notice the word "Passion": it means something done
to him, as opposed to something that he did. Christ was thought to
be entirely undeserving of the humiliation, pain and public execution—that is obvious. He was also thought to find these experiences
difficult and painful in the extreme. If we supposed that his divinity
allowed him to undergo the crucifixion without unpleasantness, we
would not be moved. He wishes that the cup might be passed from
him, and on the cross he fears, just for a moment, that his Father has
forsaken him. And the fact that Christ suffers this though he deserved
nothing but good—he is pictured as more innocent, more deserving
of good than any of us ever could be—is believed to reprieve the rest
of us from guilt. *We* are more innocent for *his* having suffered inno-
cently.

*   *   *

A moral story, such as Aristotle demands, is perhaps just what we
do *not* want. We are all much too aware that everything that we do
has consequences—and consequences that we will perhaps regret,
wretched consequences, it may be, for which we shall know that we
have only ourselves to blame. We are indeed quite willing to believe
that we may be in the dark and missing all the opportunities. We suspect, deep in our hearts, that, however much we may complain about
bad luck or ill treatment, we probably always brought on ourselves
every misery we suffer. Psychoanalysis, indeed, has discovered a whole
world of fantasy memories causing feelings of guilt that have only a
grotesque relation to what we have really done or deserve. Justice—in
the sense that punishments fit crimes or that all catastrophes stem
from serious flaws of character or understanding—is something we

suspect is true but wish were not. Proof that we need *not* accept this constant burden of self-condemnation because there really is such a thing as *in*justice, entirely unmerited misery—that is the interesting thing. We apparently find it very hard to believe in our own innocence, and cannot accept the innocence of people too like ourselves. But give us a Christ, or a Job or Antigone or Prince Mishkin or Jude the Obscure, then maybe we can believe it—just for a minute, anyhow.

Erich Fromm

Was Freud justified in concluding that this myth confirms his view that unconscious incestuous drives and the resulting hate against the father-rival are to be found in any male child? Indeed, it does seem as if the myth confirmed Freud's theory that the Oedipus complex justifiably bears its name.

If we examine the myth more closely, however, questions arise which cast some doubts on the correctness of this view. The most pertinent question is this: If Freud's interpretation is right, we should expect the myth to tell us that Oedipus met Jocasta without knowing that she was his mother, fell in love with her, and then killed his father, again unknowingly. But there is no indication whatsoever in the myth that Oedipus is attracted by or falls in love with Jocasta. The only reason we are given for Oedipus' marriage to Jocasta is that she, as it were, goes with the throne. Should we believe that a myth the central theme of which constitutes an incestuous relationship between mother and son would entirely omit the element of attraction between the two? This question is all the more weighty in view of the fact that, in the older versions of the oracle, the prediction of the marriage to the mother is mentioned only once in Nikolaus of Damascus' description, which according to Carl Robert goes back to a relatively new source.[1]

Furthermore, Oedipus is described as the courageous and wise hero who becomes the benefactor of Thebes. How can we understand that the same Oedipus is described as having committed the crime most horrible in the eyes of his contemporaries? This question has sometimes been answered by pointing to the fact that it is the very essence of the Greek concept of tragedy that it is the powerful and strong who

From Erich Fromm, *"The Oedipus Complex and the Oedipus Myth,"* in The Family: Its Function and Destiny, *Revised Edition,* ed. *Ruth Nanda Anshen, Science of Culture Series, V (New York: Harper & Row, Publishers, 1959), pp. 337-39. Copyright 1949 by Harper & Row, Publishers. Copyright © 1959 by Ruth Nanda Anshen. Reprinted by permission of Harper & Row, Publishers.*

[1] Cf. Carl Robert, *Oidipus* (Berlin: Weidmannsche Buchhandlung, 1915).

are suddenly struck by disaster. Whether such an answer is sufficient or whether another view can give us a more satisfactory answer remains to be seen.

The foregoing questions arise from a consideration of *King Oedipus*. If we examine only this tragedy, without taking into account the two other parts of the trilogy, *Oedipus at Colonus* and *Antigone,* no definite answer can be given. But we are at least in the position of formulating a hypothesis, namely *that the myth can be understood as a symbol not of the incestuous love between mother and son but of the rebellion of the son against the authority of the father in the patriarchal family; that the marriage of Oedipus and Jocasta is only a secondary element, only one of the symbols of the son's victory who takes his father's place and with it all his privileges.*

The validity of this hypothesis can be tested by examining the whole Oedipus myth, particularly in the form presented by Sophocles in the two other parts of his trilogy, *Oedipus at Colonus* and *Antigone.*[2]

In *Oedipus at Colonus* we find Oedipus near Athens at the grove of the Eumenides shortly before he dies. After having blinded himself, Oedipus had remained in Thebes, which was ruled by Creon, his uncle, who after some time exiled him. Oedipus' two daughters, Antigone and Ismene, accompanied him into exile; but his two sons, Eteocles and Polyneices, refused to help their blind father. After his departure, the two brothers strove for possession of the throne. Eteocles won; but Polyneices, refusing to yield, sought to conquer the city with outside help and to wrest the power from his brother. In *Oedipus at Colonus* we see him approach his father, begging his forgiveness and asking his assistance. But Oedipus is relentless in his hate against his sons. In spite of the passionate pleading of Polyneices, supported by Antigone's plea, he refuses forgiveness. His last words to his son are:

And thou—begone, abhorred of me, and unfathered!—begone, thou vilest of the vile, and with thee take these my curses which I call down on thee—never to vanquish the land of thy race, no, nor ever return to hill-girt Argos, but by a kindred hand to die, and slay him by whom thou hast been driven out. Such is my prayer; and I call the paternal darkness of dread Tartarus to take thee unto another home,—I call the spirits of this place,—I call the Destroying God, who hath set that dreadful hatred in you twain. Go, with these words in thine ears—go, and

---

[2] While it is true that the trilogy was not written in this order and while some scholars may be right in their assumption that Sophocles did not plan the three tragedies as a trilogy, the three must nevertheless be interpreted as a whole. It makes little sense to assume that Sophocles described the fate of Oedipus and his children in three tragedies without having in mind an inner coherence of the whole.

publish it to the Cadmeans all, yea, and to thine own staunch allies, that Oedipus hath divided such honours to his sons.[3]

In *Antigone* we find another father-son conflict as one of the central themes of the tragedy. Here Creon, the representative of the authoritarian principle in state and family, is opposed by his son, Haemon, who reproaches him for his ruthless despotism and his cruelty against Antigone. Haemon tries to kill his father and, failing to do so, kills himself.

We find that the theme which runs through the three tragedies is the conflict between father and son. In *King Oedipus*, Oedipus kills his father Laius who had intended to take the infant's life. In *Oedipus at Colonus* Oedipus gives vent to his intense hate against his sons, and in *Antigone* we find the same hate again between Creon and Haemon. The problem of incest exists neither in the relationship between Oedipus' sons to their mother nor in the relationship between Haemon and his mother, Eurydice. If we interpret *King Oedipus* in the light of the whole trilogy, the assumption seems plausible that the real issue in *King Oedipus*, too, is the conflict between father and son and not the problem of incest.

Theodore Thass-Thienemann

The Sphinx with a "female-male" winged body belongs to the same stock of imagination as do the other mythical monsters that are guardians of hidden treasures; however, the Sphinx appears to be a unique variant, comparable only to the fiery Archangel with the sword guarding the Tree of Life, which is in Paradise beside the Tree of Knowledge. The hidden treasures of the monster are not of gold. The fabulous treasure is in this special case an intellectual one: knowledge. The hidden and closely guarded secret is the Unknown of the sexual riddle. While the dragon must be killed in the other stories in order that the treasure may become the possession of man, the Sphinx significantly kills herself when her secret is broken in time of maturation. Oedipus, the swollen-footed hero, does not kill the monster by physical force but defeats her through insight and knowledge. The primary

---

From Theodore Thass-Thienemann, "Oedipus—Identity and Knowledge," Part II of The Subconscious Language (New York: Washington Square Press, Inc., 1967), pp. 93–94 and 97. Copyright © 1967 by Theodore Thass-Thienemann. Reprinted by permission of Washington Square Press, Inc.

[3] "Oedipus at Colonus," in *The Complete Greek Drama*, ed. by Whitney J. Oates and Eugene O'Neill, Jr., I (New York: Random House, 1938), ll. 1383 ff.

anxiety, connected with the sexual riddle, shapes the pattern of all
subsequent anxiety arising from the Unknown, especially if one is
confronted with the riddle of existence and nonexistence. The dragon
killer is a hero if he is the victor in the struggle with his own monster
—with the feeling of anxiety and guilt that lies hidden in his unconscious fantasies. The psychological wisdom of these mythical fantasies
consists in the insight that the unveiling of the riddle as well as the
acquisition of the hidden treasure is, in the final analysis, detrimental
for man. A curse lies upon this knowledge which is derived in one
part from acquisitiveness, in the other part from inquisitiveness. This
curse is stronger than the victorious hero. All dragon-killer heroes become finally the victims of their victory over unconscious fantasies.
Oedipus, just because he has defeated the monster of the Unknown,
personifies, we shall see, the greatest blunder, the final defeat of the
conscious self-evident thinking and the victory of the Sphinx, i.e., of
the psychic forces which are hidden in the Unconscious and the Unknown of the own self. He is the victim of his infatuation.

*   *   *

Oedipus blinds himself. Freud has pointed out that this blinding
stands for the only logical self-punishment, castration. The eyes are
as precious to man as are the genitals. One may expand this interpretation by stating that Oedipus retaliates upon the eyes not only the
epistemological mistake in genitalia (both being organs of knowledge),
but he avenges also on the outside eye the blindness of the inner eye.
What was the sense of those carnal eyes when they saw and did not
perceive? This is what Oedipus says in blinding himself: "You were
too long blind for those I was looking for." The same implication is
present in the words of Christ stating that adultery can be committed
not only by the genitals but also by the eyes; consequently to pluck
out the eyes is tantamount to castration.

George Thomson

It is necessary to remember the limitations of a society [i.e. Athenian society] called democratic in which a large and increasing section
of the community had no rights at all. The industrial exploitation of
slave-labour, which had brought the middle class to power, rapidly pro-
moted a fresh concentration of wealth in the hands of those who had

From the editor's Introduction to The Oresteia of Aeschylus, *ed. George Thomson, 1st ed., I (Cambridge: Cambridge University Press, 1938), 70–73. Copyright
1938 by Cambridge University Press. Reprinted, with omission of footnotes, by
permission of the publisher.*

the capital to exploit it. Of those who had not, the poorer metics were reduced to a condition described later as "limited slavery," while the poorer citizens, rather than succumb to this destructive competition, used their political rights to make their maintenance a charge in various forms upon the state. The charge was met in the only way it could be met without expropriating the rich—by exploiting other peoples; and, though Pericles might clothe it in fine words, the imperialist policy on which he depended for popular support meant that liberty was to be maintained at home by suppressing it abroad. "In whatever terms the powerful enjoin obedience," so Athenian democrats told the people of Melos, "to those the weak are obliged to submit." The wheel had come full circle.

In the art of tragedy these developments were indirectly but faithfully reflected.

*   *   *

The Oedipus of Sophocles is the tragic symbol of the human will struggling helplessly against a force that it cannot control or understand—a mirror of the deep-seated perplexity engendered in men's minds by the transformation of a social order designed to establish liberty and equality into an instrument for the destruction of liberty and equality. As Aristotle perceived, the function of this kind of tragedy was cathartic. The emotional stresses set up by social frustration are relieved by a spectacle in which the contradiction between the individual and society is sublimated as a conflict between man and God or Fate or Necessity.

Richmond Y. Hathorn

What is Oedipus' *hamartia* then? Obviously it is not bad temper, suspiciousness, hastiness in action—for his punishment does not fit these crimes; not ignorance of who his parents are—for ignorance of this type is not culpable; still less murder and incest—for these things are fated for him by the gods.

No, Oedipus' blind spot is his failure in existential commitment; a failure to recognize his own involvement in the human condition, a failure to realize that not all difficulties are riddles, to be solved by the application of disinterested intellect, but that some are mysteries, not to be solved at all, but to be coped with only by the engagement, ac-

From Richmond Y. Hathorn, Tragedy, Myth, and Mystery (Bloomington: Indiana University Press, 1962), p. 87. Copyright © 1962 by Indiana University Press. Reprinted, with omission of footnotes, by permission of the publisher.

tive or passive, of the whole self. Oedipus' punishment, then, is not really punishment at all, but the only means by which the gods may enlighten blindness of such density. Sophocles was not concerned to tell a crime-and-punishment story; this is shown by his leaving the "crimes" out of the action.

Richard B. Sewall

Why did Oedipus put out his eyes? Like Job's action it has "magnitude" and is heavy with ambiguities. The scene which the Messenger reports is the most horrible and the most enigmatic of the play: Oedipus snatching the brooches from the bodice of his dead wife and plunging them "from full arm's length" into his eyes, "time and time again,"

> Till bloody tears rain down his beard—not drops
> But in full spate a whole cascade descending
> In drenching cataracts of scarlet ruin.

Why this fearful image? Its surface function in the play is relatively clear. It fulfills the prophecy of Teiresias that "He that came seeing, blind shall he go," clinching the ironic theme of the blind Seer who could not, and the King who would not, see. Its very horror shows the ironic inadequacy of the Chorus' final response. Oedipus' own motives are far from clear. He says that he did it to spare himself the sight of the ugliness he had caused, that he could not bring himself to face the people on whom he had brought such suffering. In *Oedipus at Colonus* he tells his son that he did it in a moment of frenzy and not from a sense of guilt. When the Chorus, in the present play, asks him directly why he did it, he says that Apollo had a hand in it. Again, he says he did it so that he might not meet eye-to-eye his father or his mother "beyond the grave." No one reason suffices, nor all of them put together. The act seems compounded of opposite elements: egotism and altruism, self-loathing and self-glorification. As an act of destruction, it shows man at his worst. To the extent that it was "determined," it shows the gods at their worst. But as an act of freedom, it turns out to be curiously creative in unexpected ways, and shows man at his best. What Oedipus insists upon in his reply to the Chorus is that the act was his own:

> Apollo, friends, Apollo,
> Has laid this agony upon me;
> Not by his hand; I did it.

From Richard B. Sewall, The Vision of Tragedy (New Haven: Yale University Press, 1959), pp. 40–41. Copyright © 1959 by Yale University Press, Inc. Reprinted by permission of the publisher.

Whatever he may have thought he was doing, the act stands in the play as his culminating act of freedom, the assertion of his ability to act independent of any god, oracle, or prophecy.

Marshall McLuhan

In any medium or structure there is what Kenneth Boulding calls a "break boundary at which the system suddenly changes into another or passes some point of no return in its dynamic processes," [e.g.] the one from stasis to motion, and from the mechanical to the organic in the pictorial world. One effect of the static photo had been to suppress the conspicuous consumption of the rich, but the effect of the speed-up of the photo had been to provide fantasy riches for the poor of the entire globe.

Today the road beyond its break boundary turns cities into highways, and the highway proper takes on a continuous urban character. Another characteristic reversal after passing a road break boundary is that the country ceases to be the center of all work, and the city ceases to be the center of leisure. . . .

In the ancient world the intuitive awareness of break boundaries as points of reversal and of no return was embodied in the Greek idea of *hubris*, which Toynbee presents in his *Study of History*, under the head of "The Nemesis of Creativity" and "The Reversal of Roles." The Greek dramatists presented the idea of creativity as creating, also, its own kind of blindness, as in the case of Oedipus Rex, who solves the riddle of the Sphinx. It was as if the Greeks felt that the penalty for one break-through was a general sealing-off of awareness to the total field.

From Marshall McLuhan, Understanding Media: The Extensions of Man *(New York: McGraw-Hill Book Company, 1964), pp. 38-39. Copyright © 1964 by Marshall McLuhan. Reprinted by permission of the publisher.*

Chronology of Important Dates

Sophocles' Life	The Sophoclean Age
497–496 B.C. Sophocles born.	
490	Persian defeat at Marathon.
c. 485–84	Euripides born.
480	Persian defeat at Thermopylae, Salamis.
479	Persian defeat at Plataea.
477	Delian League established.
468 First victory in tragic competition.	
458	Aeschylus' *Oresteia* presented.
c. 456–55	Aeschylus' death.
447–32	Construction of Parthenon.
440's (?) *Ajax* presented.	
443–42 Service as imperial treasurer.	
c. 442 *Antigone* presented.	
441–40 Elected general.	
430's (?) *Trachiniae* presented.	
431	Start of Peloponnesian War between Athens and Sparta.
429	Death of Pericles.
429–25 (?) *Oedipus Rex* presented.	
428–27	Birth of Plato.
after 420 (?) *Electra* presented.	
415–13	Athens' unsuccessful expedition against Syracuse.
413 Service as special state commissioner.	
409 *Philoctetes* presented.	
c. 406	Euripides' death.

406–5	Sophocles' death.	
404		Fall of Athens and end of war.
401	*Oedipus at Colonus* presented posthumously.	
399		Socrates' death.

Notes on the Editor and Contributors

MICHAEL J. O'BRIEN, the editor, has taught Classics at Wesleyan and Yale and is now at University College, the University of Toronto. He has written *The Socratic Paradoxes and the Greek Mind.*

C. M. (SIR MAURICE) BOWRA, Warden of Wadham College, Oxford, numbers Homer, Pindar, and Sophocles among the subjects of his books.

E. R. DODDS is Regius Professor of Greek, Emeritus, at Oxford. Among his books are *The Greeks and the Irrational* and editions of Plato and Euripides.

VICTOR EHRENBERG has taught at Frankfurt, Prague, and London. He has written *The People of Aristophanes* and many books on ancient history.

FRANCIS FERGUSSON, who teaches Comparative Literature at Rutgers, has worked in the theater and written and lectured about it. He has edited plays of Shakespeare and Molière.

SIR JAMES FRAZER (1854–1941), classicist and anthropologist, edited Pausanias and Ovid but is best known for his work *The Golden Bough.*

SIGMUND FREUD (1856–1939), the father of psychoanalysis, saw in the Oedipus legend an answer to the problem of neurotic guilt, which he formulated in his theory of the "Oedipus complex."

ERICH FROMM is a psychoanalyst, lecturer, and author of such books as *The Sane Society* and *The Heart of Man.*

THOMAS GOULD, who teaches Classics at the University of Texas, has written *Platonic Love.*

RICHMOND Y. HATHORN teaches at the American University of Beirut and has recently had published *Crowell's Handbook of Classical Drama.*

WERNER JAEGER (1888–1961), who came from Germany to teach Greek at Chicago and then Harvard, had among his many publications works on Aristotle and Gregory of Nyssa.

G. M. KIRKWOOD, who teaches Classics at Cornell, has written *A Short Guide to Classical Mythology* as well as his book on Sophocles.

BERNARD M. W. KNOX, Director of the Center for Hellenic Studies in Washington, D. C., wrote *Oedipus at Thebes,* and then went on to translate the play and to publish *The Heroic Temper,* also about Sophocles.

RICHMOND LATTIMORE, who teaches Greek at Bryn Mawr, is a scholar, a poet, and a translator of Homer, Hesiod, Greek drama, and Greek lyric poetry.

116

"LONGINUS" is the name conventionally attached to the ancient author of uncertain date who wrote the Greek treatise *On the Sublime*.

MARSHALL McLUHAN, philosopher of the electric age, teaches English at St. Michael's College, the University of Toronto.

E. T. OWEN (1882–1948), who taught at University College, the University of Toronto, wrote *The Harmony of Aeschylus* and *The Story of the Iliad*.

PLUTARCH, the Greek philosopher and biographer of the first and early second centuries of our era, is best known for his *Parallel Lives*.

KARL REINHARDT (1886–1958) taught Classics at Frankfurt-am-Main and other German universities, and wrote books on Aeschylus, Posidonius, Homer, Parmenides, and Sophocles.

RICHARD B. SEWALL teaches English at Yale, where he is Master of Ezra Stiles College.

PAUL SHOREY (1857–1934) taught Greek at Bryn Mawr and Chicago, edited Horace, and wrote several works on Plato.

THEODORE THASS-THIENEMANN is affiliated with Harvard Medical School.

GEORGE D. THOMSON, Professor of Greek at Birmingham in England, has published books on Aeschylus and ancient Greek society as well as *Marxism and Poetry*.

VOLTAIRE, the eighteenth-century French philosopher and man of letters, wrote his own *Oedipus* at age nineteen.

A. J. A. WALDOCK (1898–1950), of the University of Sydney, Australia, wrote books on *Hamlet* and *Paradise Lost* before turning to Sophocles.

T. B. L. WEBSTER, who teaches Greek at the University of London, has written books on Homer, Menander, Sophocles, and Euripides.

R. P. WINNINGTON–INGRAM, a classicist at the University of London, has written *Euripides and Dionysus,* a study of the *Bacchae*.

Selected Bibliography

Translations (all available in paperback)

David Grene's translation can be found in several collections, among them *The Complete Greek Tragedies* (paperback edition), ed. David Grene and Richmond Lattimore, *Sophocles I* (Chicago, 1954).

Bernard M. W. Knox, *Oedipus the King* (New York, 1959).

E. F. Watling, *Sophocles, the Theban Plays*, Penguin Classics (Harmondsworth, 1947).

Criticism: Books

C. M. (Sir Maurice) Bowra, *Sophoclean Tragedy* (Oxford, 1944).

Victor Ehrenberg, *Sophocles and Pericles* (Oxford, 1954).

G. M. Kirkwood, *A Study of Sophoclean Drama* (Ithaca, 1958).

Bernard M. W. Knox, *Oedipus at Thebes* (New Haven and London, 1957).

Cedric H. Whitman, *Sophocles, a Study of Heroic Humanism* (Cambridge, Mass., 1951).

Of these, Kirkwood concentrates on dramatic art and structure, Ehrenberg emphasizes the poet's political and religious views, and Knox is particularly good on language and imagery. Knox, Bowra, and Whitman also discuss Sophocles' thought and its relation to Greek ideas and culture. The clash of views is sharpest between Bowra and Whitman. Knox and Bowra are available in paperback.

Criticism: Articles

Philip W. Harsh, "Implicit and Explicit in the *Oedipus Tyrannus*," *American Journal of Philology* 79 (1958), 243–58.

W. C. Helmbold, "The Paradox of the *Oedipus*," *American Journal of Philology* 72 (1951), 293–300.

Bernard M. W. Knox, "Why is Oedipus called Tyrannus?", *Classical Journal* 50 (1954–55), 97–102.

Bernard M. W. Knox, "The Date of the *Oedipus Tyrannus* of Sophocles," *American Journal of Philology* 77 (1956), 133–47.

Herbert Musurillo, "Sunken Imagery in Sophocles' *Oedipus*," *American Journal of Philology* 78 (1957), 36–51.

Line-by-Line Commentaries

Sir Richard C. Jebb, *Sophocles: I, The Oedipus Tyrannus,* 3rd ed. (Cambridge, 1893). This edition also has the Greek text and a translation.

J. C. Kamerbeek, *The Plays of Sophocles: Part IV, The Oedipus Tyrannus* (Leiden, 1967).

Bibliography

H. F. Johansen, "Sophocles 1939–1959," *Lustrum* 7 (1962), pp. 94–288. This contains lists, summaries, and evaluations.

TWENTIETH CENTURY
INTERPRETATIONS
MAYNARD MACK, *Series Editor*
Yale University

NOW AVAILABLE
Collections of Critical Essays
ON

ADVENTURES OF HUCKLEBERRY FINN
ALL FOR LOVE
ARROWSMITH
AS YOU LIKE IT
THE BOOK OF JOB
THE CASTLE
THE DUCHESS OF MALFI
EURIPIDES' ALCESTIS
THE FROGS
GRAY'S ELEGY
THE GREAT GATSBY
GULLIVER'S TRAVELS
HAMLET
HENRY IV, PART TWO
HENRY V
THE ICEMAN COMETH
JULIUS CAESAR
KEATS'S ODES
OEDIPUS REX
THE PORTRAIT OF A LADY
A PORTRAIT OF THE ARTIST AS A YOUNG MAN
SAMSON AGONISTES
THE SCARLET LETTER
SIR GAWAIN AND THE GREEN KNIGHT

THE SOUND AND THE FURY
TOM JONES
TWELFTH NIGHT
UTOPIA
WALDEN
THE WASTE LAND
WUTHERING HEIGHTS